COVERING

the Campus

COVERING

the Campus

THE HISTORY
OF
THE CHRONICLE
of Higher Education.

1966-1993

PATRICIA BALDWIN

University of North Texas Press

Denton, Texas

Requests for permission to reproduce material from this work
should be sent to:

Permissions
University of North Texas Press
P. O. Box 13856
Denton, Texas 76203

The paper used in this book meets the minimum requirements of the
American National Standard for Permanence of Paper for Printed Library
materials, Z39.48.1984

Library of Congress Cataloging–in–Publication Data

Baldwin, Patricia L., 1949–
Covering the campus: the history of The chronicle of higher education / by
Patricia L. Baldwin.
p.   cm.
Includes bibliographical references and index.
ISBN 0-929398-96-3 (cloth : alk. paper).–ISBN 0-929398-97-1
(paper : alk. paper)
1. Chronicle of higher education–History. I. Title. LB2300.B35 1995
378'.05–dc20   95-8936
CIP

Design by Amy Layton

TABLE OF CONTENTS

XV. APPENDICES

XVI. REFERENCES

LIST OF TABLES

PREFACE

When I met Corbin Gwaltney in June 1992 to propose this manuscript, he said he had been too busy over the years, working as a "plain ol' reporter," to have compiled a history of *The Chronicle of Higher Education.* Still, the newspaper had marked its twenty-fifth anniversary the previous November and the story melded a quarter-century of higher education and journalism milestones. The time had come to record those milestones.

The difficulty in such a task is that *The Chronicle* is an ever-changing entity and a manuscript must have an end. Thus, this book focuses on the first quarter-century of *The Chronicle*, with dates and figures updated as best as possible to reflect the newspaper's evolution into its twenty-seventh year. Since completion of this manuscript in late 1993, *The Chronicle* again has expanded its office space to occupy the entire seventh floor of the building at 1255 Twenty-Third Street, N.W. in Washington, D.C. Robin Ross has been named to the long-vacant publisher's post. The publication has greatly expanded its editorial services via the Internet. And it continues to raise the bar on its journalistic mission.

What has not changed is Corbin Gwaltney's enthusiasm for his weekly journalistic endeavor, his constant challenging of himself and others, his quest for invention, and his desire for perfection. The editor is a connoisseur of change.

For his cooperation and that of his staff, I am grateful. This manuscript represents many trips to Washington and elsewhere, hours of taped interviews, and additional hours of reporting and research on the telephone, in libraries across the country, and at *The Chronicle*'s offices. In addition the support of *The Dallas Morning News*—WFAA Foundation was instrumental in the completion of this project and is acknowledged with sincere appreciation. Finally, I appreciate the confidence of Fran Vick and her staff at the University of North Texas Press. By publishing this book, they have contributed a legacy to the very different worlds of journalism and academe.

Patricia C. Baldwin
September, 1995

CHAPTER I

SHOOTING FOR THE MOON: THE EARLY DAYS

Editorial Projects in Education

Corbin Gwaltney handed over a nickel for a copy of the *New York Times*. He had only intended to catch a quick breath of fresh air after breakfast, before the select group of twelve university alumni magazine editors reconvened the day's meetings. But as the editor from Johns Hopkins University stepped from the lobby of the Dupont Plaza Hotel and walked toward the traffic circle, already busy with early morning Washington commuters, the October 5, 1957, banner headline caught his attention. The all-cap letters delivered the historic news:

SOVIET FIRES EARTH SATELLITE INTO SPACE;
IT IS CIRCLING THE GLOBE AT 18,000 M.P.H.;
SPHERE TRACKED IN 4 CROSSINGS OVER U.S.

"They're shooting for the moon," commented one of Gwaltney's fellow editors upon seeing the newspaper (Gwaltney, 1992a).

"So are we," retorted Gwaltney (1992a), who, at thirty-five, was already considered the dean of alumni publishing, having transformed *The Johns Hopkins Magazine*, as one colleague described, "from a dreary rag to a model of photojournalism" (Cleveland, 1991, p. 95).

Thus, as the first Sputnik circled the earth, "Moonshooter" was christened. Designed as a shared supplement to be bound into a small group of university alumni magazines, the first thirty-two-page *Moonshooter Report*, entitled "U.S. Higher Education 1958," was an attempt by a core dozen editors to "lift our eyes above the fences that surrounded higher education generally," Gwaltney remembered (1992a). For funding, each editor pledged sixty percent of the budget from one issue of his or her alumni publication. Almost as an afterthought, the group offered the supplement to other alumni magazine editors, and, to their amazement, 150 universities bought 1,350,000 copies at a nickel a copy.

For the second year of the *Moonshooter*, the group obtained a $12,500 grant from the Carnegie Corporation of New York. Again, the editors offered their report to colleagues, who responded with orders for 2,250,000 copies. The "Moonshooters" sent back the $12,500 to the Carnegie Corporation with a note saying, in essence, thanks, we do not need your money after all.

One of the alumni editors assessed the venture in a letter:

> A group of editors banding together in a common belief in American higher education and in a common desire to tell its story in a way that has never been tried before will in itself have an impact that no one of us could hope to achieve alone. . . . Out of this beginning can grow something tremendously important (Wolk, 1992, p. 1).

The words were prophetic. Circulation the third year surpassed three million, reaching alumni at more than three hundred universities. The part-time effort was transforming into a full-time job. In 1961, Gwaltney volunteered to quit his post at Johns Hopkins to become the first full-time employee of the newly formed Editorial Projects for Education (EPE), later renamed Editorial Projects in Education. From a desk in Gwaltney's Baltimore apartment, the venture soon graduated to an office near the Johns Hopkins campus.

"We had talent and assets. The question was what else we ought to be doing," said Ronald A. Wolk (1993), who was the volunteer chairman of Editorial Projects for Education at the time and who had succeeded Gwaltney as the Johns Hopkins alumni editor.

Editorial Projects for Education decided to survey the higher education community regarding its need for information. Wolk took a leave of absence from his post at Johns Hopkins and, with a $25,000 grant from the Carnegie Corporation, traveled the country for eight months, talking to educators at all levels. The resulting report outlined the status of the dissemination of information about higher education. The document analyzed audiences; it assessed the quality of work being done by mass media education writers.

"We pointed to a great lack of understanding by the general public—indeed, by the people in the field themselves—about the real issues in higher education," Wolk (1993) said. "One of the recommendations was for a communication vehicle for college and university trustees."

Wolk's report for the Carnegie Corporation pointed out:

> Members of the horse-racing fraternity, fans of baseball, investors in stocks receive complete daily statistics within hours, a number of persons reminded us, while persons in education must wait for months, and sometimes years, for the data they need (Wolk, 1963. p. 33).

Editorial Projects successfully petitioned the Carnegie Corporation for $68,500 for a newsletter for trustees, first issued on February 5, 1965, called the *15-Minute Report*. Gwaltney became editor and also began syndicating news and feature articles, written by the likes of Margaret Mead and Bertrand Russell, which were distributed to alumni magazines.

"As we published, we became very aware that among the most faithful readers of the *15-Minute Report* were college and university administrators," Gwaltney (1992a) said. "The light bulb went on that higher education generally would benefit from a news publication."

The Chronicle's Launch

They did not call it a "newspaper" at first. After all, the academic community had little use for journalists and seemingly had enough scholarly publications and newsletters of its own. During a visit by Wolk to Chatham College in Pittsburgh, Pennsylvania, the president had lifted a Campbell's Soup box off his desk. The box was filled with publications.

"I take one of these home practically every night," the president told Wolk (1993). But the hands-on, entrepreneurial Editorial Projects board envisioned a publication that would make a lot of the existing reading material unnecessary. They sketched out a plan for *The Chronicle of Higher Education.*

Consultant Alan Pifer, who became president of the Carnegie Corporation of New York in 1965, said his organization agreed that a "message center" (1993) was needed in higher education following the expansionary periods of the 1950s and 1960s. However, some at the Carnegie Corporation were quite leery of financing the project, he recalled. The hesitancy did not exist because of any risk factor.

On the contrary, Pifer (1993) said, "That never stopped us. We were in the business of supporting risky things. I felt that was what foundations were for." But others felt that Gwaltney was being closed-mouth about the true journalistic intent of the project, or, in other words, that the ultimate goal was to start a mass circulation newspaper.

"They thought his plans were larger really than he had let on," Pifer said (1993). With hindsight, of course, the plans *were* larger than Gwaltney had let on—perhaps because he had not realized the magnitude of the undertaking himself, worrying mainly about filling a biweekly's eight pages. Pifer prevailed, however, and the Carnegie Corporation backed the tabloid with a two-year grant of $120,000, paid in equal annual installments. On November 23, 1966, *The Chronicle of Higher Education* made its debut.

Although its benefactors eventually recognized that *The Chronicle* filled an important information gap in American higher education, a later proposal by the Editorial Projects board for a counterpart publication for secondary education was not funded by the Carnegie Corporation, Pifer said, reflecting the foundation community's apparent misgivings about being in the newspaper business. More than a decade later, however, the Carnegie Corporation did participate in the funding of *Education Week*, founded by the renamed Editorial Projects in Education for the elementary and secondary school audiences.

Early Decisions

The early foundation support provided enough financial comfort for Gwaltney and *The Chronicle*'s start-up staff to shape a distinctive publication philosophy. Two decisions, in particular, marked the newspaper as a publishing anomaly. The newspaper had no advertising and no staff-written editorial opinions.

The fact that the publication eschewed all advertising at the beginning was characteristic of Gwaltney's high-road attitude about journalism. The editor said he felt that advertising might compromise the newspaper. Editorial Projects chairman Wolk added that, although he did not believe it, the editor might have felt *The Chronicle* could not attract sufficient commercial support.

Whatever the case, the decision turned out to be a beneficial strategy because before too long, advertisers were beating down the proverbial door. Later, of course, advertising, especially the paper's hefty classified jobs section, catapulted *The Chronicle* to financial independence. Indeed, after nearly a quarter of a century, *Bulletin Board* job listings composed the major international job marketplace for higher education.

The decision to avoid advocacy journalism was rooted in Gwaltney's belief that academics are a most critical audience, composed of people trained in marshalling facts and coming to their own conclusions. Thus, *The Chronicle* has offered lively debate on issues, but strictly through its letters, opinion, and *Point of View* pieces contributed mostly by its higher education constituents. Gwaltney's confidence in the validity of the "no editorials" decision has never wavered.

"We decided to be absolutely straight arrow in covering the news of higher education," Gwaltney (1992a) said. "There was no point in launching *The Chronicle of Higher Education* if it were not conceived on the highest principles of journalism."

Response corroborated the actions. Gwaltney credited the early decisions for the newspaper's fairly immediate acceptance in terms of circulation and feedback from readers. Adding to the success was an initial ten-dollar subscription rate, quite inexpensive in comparison to specialized higher education journals and newsletters. That is not to say the newspaper ever shied away from controversy. Coverage of such topics as AIDS, gender-equity, and play-for-pay athletics was months, and in some cases years, ahead of the national media in its candor and explicitness. Nor were early decisions indications that Gwaltney intended to tread softly on academic egos.

In particular, the honorific of "Dr." was reserved solely for medical doctors, outraging some letter writers among the publication's readership, who were largely holders of Ph.D. degrees. Gwaltney explained (1992a) that the decision was not made lightly, and he relied on an episode from the folklore of Harvard University, an institution where it remains gauche to use "Dr." in addressing a Ph.D., to further substantiate the stance. The Harvard legend supposedly took place in the early 1900s, when Charles W. Eliot was president of the university. A man arrived unannounced at Eliot's office and asked the secretary if he could see him. "No," she replied. "The president is in Washington seeing Mr. Wilson." It was clear: the "Dr." was president and the president was "Mr."

The Start-up Team

As the story is retold, Gwaltney learned in 1949 of dissatisfaction at his alma mater, Johns Hopkins University, with its alumni magazine. Then in labor relations work for General Electric, Gwaltney judged the magazine as poorly laid out and dull in content. He drew up a dummy for a new design and sent it to the university provost.

"I had as a kid aspired to be a newspaper person," he related (1992a). "So I invented the job at Hopkins and then sold it to them. I did that because it was a way into publishing, a way into ink on paper."

From his earliest editing days, Gwaltney gained a reputation for being obsessive about quality and details. In addition to his talent for the written word and his skill in layout and design, Gwaltney has been frequently lauded, since the early days at Johns Hopkins, for his photo editing. In those days, he discovered it cost no more to hire great photographers such as *Life* magazine's Eric Hartman than to hire unknowns. The editor's cutting-edge thinking went beyond the printed page, however.

Earlier, when he designed a logo for the *Moonshooter* report, he graphically styled the two sets of double "o's" to appear as movie film canisters, suggesting the possibility of expansion into multimedia. He also coined the term "Chronicle-Plus," envisioning a quick-update medium, long before the introduction of the facsimile machine. As if they have memorized the words from a manual, staff members often repeat the same description of *The Chronicle*'s chief: "Corbin loves nothing better than a blank sheet of paper in front of him so he can create something new" (Taylor, 1992).

Second to take his place on the initial staff of twelve was John A. "Jack" Crowl, whose first title was associate editor. By 1966, Crowl had used a master's degree in history from the University of Maryland to teach for a time and had been working in the Johns Hopkins public relations office for about three years. He was admittedly restive, seeing little chance for advancement in the small office headed by a relatively young boss. Besides, he was not particularly enamored with "PR," a pastime he felt endeavored to put "a spin on everything." He had started a search for another opportunity when a "fluke" occurred (Crowl, 1993).

Editorial Projects chairman Wolk, an assistant to Johns Hopkins President Milton Eisenhower, had an office in the same building with Crowl. Wolk knew Gwaltney needed to hire someone, but had been reluctant to approach another Hopkins employee. One day, he was walking down the hall when a person delivering mail dropped a letter. Wolk picked up the envelope and noticed it was addressed to Crowl from a university that Wolk knew was looking to expand its public relations operation. He surmised Crowl was looking for another job and approached him about *The Chronicle* post.

Crowl met with Gwaltney, who subsequently offered him a job, but made the risk factor perfectly clear. "He said *The Chronicle* had a grant for two years," Crowl recalled (1993). "He said, 'If we can't make it go after two years, you're out of a job.'"

At thirty-one, Crowl had a wife and family, but decided the gamble of having to start over again was an acceptable risk. More than any other reason, he accepted the job to work with Gwaltney, who had attained a reputation for journalistic innovation during his years as an alumni magazine editor. Years later, during a household move, Crowl came across his high school yearbook. "I had written that my ambition was to be a journalist. I had forgotten all about it" (Crowl, 1993).

William A. "Bill" Miller, Jr., *The Chronicle*'s first managing editor, was known as a traditional newspaperman because of earlier employment with the *New York Herald Tribune*. Prior to his joining *The Chronicle*, he was editor of the American Council on Education's weekly newsletter, *Higher Education & National Affairs*. Miller and Gwaltney delighted in the number of articles they could literally cram onto the front page. One week's issue had eleven stories. Even after Miller left the weekly, an especially news-laden front page would be referred to, in jest, as a "Bill Miller" page.

Current managing editor Malcolm G. Scully joined the staff as a reporter nearly a year to the day after *The Chronicle*'s launch. He, too, offered a traditional journalism background as an education writer at the *Charlotte Observer*. A graduate of the University of Virginia, he earned a master's degree in English literature while on a Woodrow Wilson fellowship at Cornell University in the mid-1960s. He quickly received the title of assistant editor at *The Chronicle*.

Associate editor Edward R. "Ted" Weidlein contended he was "more of a student journalist than a student" during his days at Princeton University and his tenure as managing editor of the *Daily Princeton* (Weidlein, 1992a). After graduation in 1968, he joined the university's admissions office and discovered *The Chronicle* was a great resource for his position. His newspaper yearnings also made him target the newspaper as a prospective employer. In 1971, he was "at the right place at the right time" and joined the publication as assistant editor (Weidlein, 1992a).

Senior writer Robert L. Jacobson was not long out of City College of New York, where he edited the school newspaper, when he signed on to be among the reporters listed in *The Chronicle*'s first issue. He left in the 1970s for a brief stint with the Education Commission of the State of Colorado, but returned to *The Chronicle* where he continued his specialized writing duties as *The Chronicle* marked its twenty-seventh anniversary.

Also among longtime staffers is Cheryl M. Fields, who joined the Washington bureau in 1970 and became associate managing editor for *Point of View & Opinion* in the fall of 1988. Edith "Dedie" Uunila Taylor, who joined the newspaper in 1970, has shaped the publication's library and research operations and guided the development of *Gazette*. Philip W. "Phil" Semas became assistant editor in 1969 after serving as a stringer on the West Coast. A University of Oregon journalism graduate, he served as managing editor for ten years prior to becoming founding editor of *The Chronicle of Philanthropy*, a companion publication launched in 1988.

A poster created to commemorate *The Chronicle*'s twenty-fifth anniversary in 1991 listed every staff member of the newspaper, according to the year he or she joined. A total of 496 people had worked at *The Chronicle* in its first twenty-five years, with some alumni moving on to such journalistic organizations as CBS News, *Time*, the *Washington Post*, *Harper's*, the *New York Times*, the *Los Angeles Times*, *Esquire*, the *Congressional Quarterly*, and the *Wall Street Journal*.

CHAPTER II

ROUGH PROOFS:
THE GROWING YEARS

Survival Tactics

Cigarette burns obliterated some of the numbers on Ron Wolk's yellow, lined tablet. The figures plotted the demise of *The Chronicle of Higher Education* and how the Editorial Projects for Education board would pay off the staff and get out of its office rent. The year was 1969, the same year the newspaper went weekly, and the publication edged toward the possibility of bankruptcy because of Editorial Projects for Education's inability to obtain tax-exempt status. Without the 501(c)(3) designation, the tax-reform act of 1968 had made it virtually impossible for non-exempt groups to gain foundation grants. A third try for tax-exempt status, by a new group of lawyers hired by Editorial Projects, succeeded just in time. A $350,000 Ford Foundation grant was cleared, and *The Chronicle* continued publishing—and growing.

The former physician's office in the handsome old brick townhouse on the corner of 33rd and Charles Street across from Johns Hopkins University in Baltimore had been comfortable, if a bit cozy, when Gwaltney and Crowl were just issuing the *15-Minute Report* and the *Moonshooter* inserts. With *The Chronicle*'s launch, however, the operation hired additional staff—and needed more space. The floor was crowded, with a pediatrician across the hall and a urologist next door. The two editors nosed around the building's basement, which was being used for storage, and decided to approach the landlord with a proposition. They agreed to pay another $100, the amount of rent for the upstairs suite, for use of the unfinished, but roomier, downstairs area.

"We did not have to move, so it kind of made sense," Crowl said (Crowl, 1993). On the upside, they could still use the library at neighboring Johns Hopkins, but they also had to climb up and down the stairs between the two connecting parts of the office. Managing editor Scully especially harbors not-so-fond memories of the basement newsroom. At six-foot, five-inches, Scully frequently grazed the top of his head along the pipes running across the low, exposed ceiling.

After nearly four years in the upstairs-downstairs arrangement, the newspaper again needed to expand and could find no good reason, other than it was Gwaltney's hometown, to stay in Baltimore. Crowl took the search for accommodations to Washington, D.C., where he leased about six thousand square feet in an office building owned by Georgetown University and restricted to non-profit organizations. Thus, 1717 Massachusetts Avenue, N.W., became *The Chronicle*'s next address.

"The real estate agent kept saying that the biggest mistake people make when they move to Washington is not getting enough space," Crowl said (1993). "He was right." The publication later expanded from the Massachusetts Avenue location to offices at 1333 New Hampshire Avenue. In 1985, *The Chronicle* moved to its third Washington headquarters site, a mid-rise building at 1255 23rd Street, N.W., in the capital city's West End. The newspaper's space was expanded in late 1992 to 32,000 square feet, and the floor held future expansion potential for a total of 38,000 square feet.

The Washington move proved particularly serendipitous for *The Chronicle*. Not only is information the second-largest business in the nation's capital city, but the Higher Education Act of 1965 had given the federal government a major role in higher education. The legislation, promoted by President Lyndon Johnson, committed the federal government to the premise that no one should be denied an education because of lack of funds. With the government aid, however, came oversight, accountability, public scrutiny, paperwork, and the need for more information.

Thus, it is no coincidence that most of the higher education associations are located in Washington. Over the past quarter-century, the District of Columbia has been the destination of a steady stream of representatives from colleges and universities all over the country. They come to shake the so-called money tree and try to keep up with the regulations that affect them. From the care of laboratory animals to the disposal of hazardous materials to affirmative action, most higher education issues are talked about in Washington.

That talk has been fodder for pages within *The Chronicle*, launched just at the beginning of what was probably the most tumultuous period in higher education in this country. The first edition offered retrospective views as well as a look ahead at politics and education. The 89th Congress, which passed more higher education legislation than its eighty-eight predecessors combined (McNett, 1966, p. 1), had just adjourned. The premier issue also came on the heels of Ronald Reagan's election as governor of California, where higher education had been a major campaign issue, and where rumors ran rampant about the impending ouster of Clark Kerr, the University of California president (Reece, 1966, p. 1). In fact, just a few issues later, *The Chronicle* was reporting Kerr's dismissal, and, on the same front page, his appointment as chairman of what became known as the Carnegie Commission on Higher Education and, later, the Carnegie Council on Policy Studies in Higher Education (Gwaltney, 1967b, p. 1).

Alan Pifer, the Carnegie Corporation of New York president who recruited Kerr to his new post, said the rapidity by which Kerr's appointment came was no coincidence. The former California president had already agreed to chair the group on a part-time, voluntary basis. Pifer offered the full-time Carnegie post even before the group's membership appointments were finalized. Pifer felt, he said later, that the appointment would be Kerr's public vindication. It was that, and more. Between 1967 and 1979, the Carnegie Corporation of New York and the Carnegie Foundation for the Advancement of

Teaching spent about $12 million to support the Commission and the successor Council. The investment made possible, according to a Carnegie history, the "longest and broadest survey of higher education ever undertaken in the United States, or, for that matter, anywhere in the world" (Lagemann, 1983, p. 122).

Affirmative Action and Classified

The so-called good ol' boy network filled most of the academic positions in United States higher education well into the 1960s. In Great Britain, however, every job vacancy in academe had to be advertised, a system the egalitarian Gwaltney felt held merit. Thus, the *London Times Education Supplement* carried extensive classified advertisements. A later publication, the *Times Higher Education Supplement*, continued to advertise that it provided "the most popular source" for job vacancies in higher education (Advertisement, 1993, p. 38).

So the Editorial Projects board members were canvassed and convinced to "prime the pump," as Wolk related (Wolk, 1993). On March 23, 1970, a one-column by three-inch box appeared in *The Chronicle*. The box, labeled "Advertisement" and titled "Positions Available," carried three advertisements, two of them blind (with responses going to a box number in care of the newspaper). One ad sought applicants for the "assistant to the president" post at a private university in the Northeast. The other advertised for a financial aid officer for an accredited professional school on the East Coast. The third classified listing was placed by Indiana University of Pennsylvania for a dean of faculty and academic affairs. Growth of the advertising section progressed steadily, at best. Then came affirmative action.

Since the Civil Rights Act of 1964, federal civil rights officials had focused on upholding the ban against racial discrimination at colleges and universities that received federal assistance. Then, in early 1970, activist women's groups, on the basis of a 1968 federal executive order, began filing charges of sex discrimination against colleges and universities. In June 1970, the Labor Department issued guidelines to implement the sex discrimination ban set forth in the earlier executive order (Fields, 1971, p. A1). Colleges and universities developed affirmative action plans dealing with sex discrimination similar to the plans dealing with racial discrimination.

Within academe, also, there were calls to re-evaluate the status quo. In January, 1971, a list of eighty-five "Theses" relating to the goals and internal organization of universities was published as *A First Report of the Assembly on University Goals and Governance*. The Theses, written by a committee chaired by Martin Meyerson and Stephen R. Graubard, followed fifteen months of deliberations. Later published in *Daedalus, the Journal of the American Academy of Arts and Sciences*, which Graubard edited, No. 18 of the Theses addressed the role of advertising in academic recruiting.

> While advertising for candidates for university teaching posts is not regarded as undignified in many English-speaking countries, it is in the United States. In America, cronyism may easily substitute for a critical assessment of a wide range of available candidates. Advertising is no panacea; however, it and other means of locating candidates and soliciting their interest about posts that are open ought to be more widely used. Any device that serves to make a greater number of people aware of the existence of an academic vacancy and that disseminates information about it may help obtain better applicants (Assembly, 1975, p. 331).

Some differences of opinion exist as to whether or not the advertisements are actually effective. Wolk acknowledged (1993) that, in the early days, institutions advertised in *The Chronicle* because they had to, and they did not expect to hire anybody who responded.

"They were astonished to find they received applications from people who were really interesting," he said (Wolk, 1993). "I had that experience at Brown University (where he served as a vice president from 1969 to 1978), where we literally knew who we wanted to hire, but advertised in *The Chronicle* because we were required to. We got 120 applications and ended up hiring somebody from the pool from *The Chronicle*."

Allan Ostar (1993), a recruiter for the highest levels of higher education, is a contrarian on this point. The senior consultant for

Academic Search Consultation Service and former president of the American Association of State Colleges and Universities believes the search process, especially at the presidential level, is "more complicated" (Ostar, 1993) than issuing a classified ad.

Clark Kerr, president emeritus of the University of California, is more blunt, saying that searching for a job via a classified advertisement—at least at the presidential level—"almost has a negative impact" (Kerr, 1993). "I don't know of any place that ever took seriously the people who responded to those advertisements (for presidential candidates)," he said (Kerr, 1993).

Gwaltney conceded to Kerr's point when discussing the nation's largest universities, but he said he has had presidents from other, smaller colleges tell him that they were hired as a result of their answering a *Chronicle* classified advertisement (Gwaltney, 1993n). The argument is somewhat academic. The percent of president/chief executive officer positions is small compared with the total number of jobs advertised in any single year. For example, in 1986, only two percent, or 876, of the 43,800 positions advertised in Bulletin Board were for presidents and chief executive officers (Giusto, 1993).

Independent research conducted by Oxford College of Emory University in Oxford, Georgia, in 1987, showed *The Chronicle* to be the single most important resource that higher education administrators use to begin their personal job searches, outranking even job seekers' traditional reliance on colleagues, friends, and networking. In addition, thirty percent of the national sample made up of 366 administrators at every level said very specifically that they first found out about the job they currently held through *The Chronicle*'s advertising (Molins and Martin, 1987). Additional results of the survey included:

1. twenty-four percent of those surveyed said that they found out about their current job through friends and networking;
2. another twenty percent said that they were either recruited or invited to apply for their present job;
3. thirteen percent found out about their job through other word-of-mouth contacts or from internal job postings; and,

4. only twelve percent said that they found their present job through a placement service.

The results surprised even the researchers. In a letter to Gwaltney, dated December 16, 1987, researchers Molins and Martin reported, "Frankly, we were somewhat startled by the evidence that job seekers seem to rely so heavily on *The Chronicle*. We had initially felt that our survey might uncover what we believed to have been the widespread belief that the majority of ads listing positions in *The Chronicle* represent jobs for which no real searches are to be conducted. Apparently, such is not the case."

No doubt, *The Chronicle* benefited from the spirit of the law as well as the letter. *Bulletin Board* reached a full page in the January 31, 1972, issue. The section hit 102 pages January 3, 1990, *Bulletin Board*'s largest year in *The Chronicle*'s first quarter-century, with 2,684 pages compared with 1,908 five years earlier. With its 1990 performance in classified advertising, *The Chronicle* led the nation's trade periodicals in this advertising category, according to *Classified Advertising Report*. The advertising newsletter characterized the year as flat for most publishers, with the seventeen largest trade publications growing less than one percent in classified advertising (Seventeen, 1991, p. 1).

A year later, although the higher education newspaper's classified volume dropped nearly nineteen percent, *The Chronicle* still led the nation's nineteen largest trade periodicals, which dropped 17.9 percent in overall classified advertising in 1991, according to the *Electronic Directory & Classified Report* (Classified, 1992, p. 1). Table 1 shows the growth of *The Chronicle*'s classified advertising from 1982, when the newspaper began tracking the number of individual classified placements, to 1992. Table 2 shows classified advertising volume for the top trade periodicals (the only publications to surpass 1,000 pages in annual volume) for the years 1989–1991.

TABLE 1
CLASSIFIED ADVERTISING PAGES AND ADVERTISEMENT INSERTIONS, 1982-1992

Year	Pages	Advertisement Insertions
1982	1,257	26,999
1983	1,397	27,759
1984	1,706	33,680
1985	1,908	35,564
1986	1,953	34,731
1987	2,014	36,986
1988	2,397	38,719
1989	2,610	39,217
1990	2,684	39,235
1991	2,182	30,616
1992	2,128	29,071

Source: *The Chronicle of Higher Education.*
Note: Classified advertisements may include more than one listed position.

TABLE 2
CLASSIFIED ADVERTISING PAGES AT LEADING TRADE PERIODICALS, 1989-1991

| Periodical | Classified Pages | | |
	1989	1990	1991
The Chronicle of Higher Education	2,610	2,684	2,182
Computer Reseller News	1,383	1,589	1,391
New England Journal of Medicine	1,093	1,127	1,010

Source: Communications Trends Inc., Larchmont, NY.

Independence

Less than a decade after Editorial Projects for Education saved *The Chronicle* from extinction, it equally struggled with the publication's success. The newspaper's profitability generated enough unrelated business income to threaten the non-profit group's tax-exempt status. A sense of monotony for board members had also set in, with Wolk remembering that every meeting seemed to end with Gwaltney showing slides and charts illustrating how successful *The Chronicle* had become.

"We were even meeting in good hotels," he said with a laugh (Wolk, 1993). "But the board wanted to keep its hands dirty." Gwaltney proposed that Editorial Projects create a new projects division and asked Wolk if he would join the group full time as a vice president.

"I said I would only come if I had autonomy—at least to a point," Wolk said (1993). "I realized Corbin would have the final say. I had been a friend for thirty years, but I did not want to go back in time and go to work for him again. And, I had, in a sense, been his boss as chairman of the (Editorial Projects) board."

The compromise was an attempt to create a closely held corporation that would pursue new projects. The Editorial Projects board consulted lawyers, who rebuffed the idea. Their legal counsel: Sell *The Chronicle*, and Editorial Projects can use the proceeds to start new projects. But Gwaltney and Wolk wanted it all, so to speak. They could not abide the thought of a publishing giant acquiring *The Chronicle*.

"We were spending more per editorial page than anybody in the country in those days," Wolk said. "We really cared about the editorial product, and we weren't trying to maintain some advertising/editorial ratio to make stockholders happy. A commercial company would have had to do that" (Wolk, 1993).

Then the lawyers offered an alternative suggestion. Sell *The Chronicle*, but sell it to the staff. Wolk and Gwaltney asked if that was legal and ethical. Wolk visited the Carnegie and Ford foundations that had supported the newspaper during its first decade. Both had the attitude that they had gotten their money's worth. The publication had more than fulfilled the terms of the original grants. Wolk was ready to leave Brown University and direct Editorial Projects in new ventures. He also believed that the people who took the initial risks, namely Gwaltney and Crowl, should benefit.

"When *The Chronicle* was just a gleam in people's eyes, these guys were willing to go out and do it, even if they had to mortgage their houses or whatever," Wolk said, "They suffered through the lean years and devoted their careers to it in the good ol' spirit of American capitalism" (Wolk, 1993).

So the Editorial Projects board went to Alex. Brown & Sons Inc. in Baltimore and told the brokerage firm to establish a fair price for *The Chronicle*. This deal was then presented to a second law firm, which was instructed to analyze it and make sure the transaction was absolutely legal and ethical. Some $35,000 in professional fees later, the deal was closed in November 1978, with Gwaltney and then executive editor Crowl forming a separate corporation to purchase the newspaper.

Terms of the transaction were approximately $2 million in cash plus another $500,000 worth of services that *The Chronicle* would render for Editorial Projects and its new projects, such as equipment and certain use of its information. Editorial Projects carried a twelve-year note at a floating interest rate of two points above prime, but with a floor of eight percent and a ceiling of thirteen percent. At the time of the sale, Gwaltney and Crowl considered themselves "deeply in debt" (Crowl, 1993). In November 1982, however, some eight years ahead of schedule, the owners paid off the debt to Editorial Projects.

After Editorial Projects' sale of *The Chronicle*, Wolk became the full-time president of the non-profit group and spent about two years determining the organization's next steps. In September 1981, Editorial Projects launched *Education Week*, somewhat a clone of *The Chronicle* for the elementary and secondary school audience. Seven years later, Editorial Projects added *Teacher Magazine* to its publication roster. Still tax-exempt and still losing money, Editorial Projects continued, in the early 1990s, to have "two or three other things still cooking," Wolk said. And while some things do not change, he noted that the "shoestring" is a little longer the second time around (Wolk, 1993).

"*The Chronicle* probably had about $600,000 total in foundation grants," Wolk said. "*Education Week* had about $3.5 to $4 million for its launch. *Teacher Magazine* had closer to $6 million. . . . It really is a miracle *The Chronicle* did not go under" (Wolk, 1993).

CHAPTER III

INDEPENDENCE: NEW RISKS PAY OFF

Expansion

Independence brought some immediate practical benefits to *The Chronicle*'s reporting staff. After more than a decade, for example, the newspaper's reporters were allowed into the House and Senate press galleries, areas banned to non-profit publications. The *New York Times* could no longer refer to the publication, as it had, as a "foundation-supported weekly." Board meetings simply meant a walk down the hall for Gwaltney or Crowl. Whether from fear or excitement, the shift to being a closely held publication energized the entire staff.

"I feel we were risk takers," Gwaltney observed. "I have always gotten a thrill out of each new risk that we take, whether it's financial or editorial or whatever" (1992c).

The growth of advertising revenue brought the resources, people and money, for the editorial product to become more ambitious. One friendly critic suggested that when a subject got too unwieldy for general news coverage, *The Chronicle* created a section. Sections, which the editors say guide the readers through the newspaper, also indicate the major areas of emphasis in higher education coverage. By the 1990s, major sections included *Scholarship, Personal and Professional, Teaching, Information Technology, Government and Politics,*

Business and Philanthropy, Athletics, International, Arts, and the *Gazette* or announcements. Other divisional headings have come and gone as the need or inspiration arose. The positioning of the *Scholarship* section at the front of the newspaper in more recent years, Gwaltney acknowledged, is an effort to increase readership among faculty members. As Table 3 shows, faculty readership increased more than forty percent in a seven-year period between 1984 and 1991.

TABLE 3
SUBSCRIBERS' JOB TITLES IN HIGHER EDUCATION

Title	1984	1987	1991
Senior administration	11.2%	15.0%	16.0%
Other business officers	21.4	38.5	32.5
Other academic officers	23.5	31.8	24.1
Faculty	23.2	30.7	32.9
Others (higher education)	7.3	13.6	12.9
Total in higher education	86.6%	85.5%	84.2%
Not in higher education	18.4	14.5	15.8
Total all subscribers*	105.0%	100.0%	100.0%

Sources: Simmons Market Research Bureau for 1984 and 1987; Globe Research Corporation for 1991.

Note: *Adds to more than 100 percent because some respondents hold more than one job.

As the newspaper expanded, *The Chronicle* carved its niche as "the essential current-awareness tool for events in academe" (Rice and Paster, 1990, p. 285). Some consider it the *Wall Street Journal* of higher education because of its combination of breaking news and feature stories as well as comprehensive data listings that used to get published slowly or were narrowly distributed (Hefferlin and Phillips, 1971).

Combined with its companion publication, *The Chronicle of Philanthropy*, *The Chronicle*'s business venture, after twenty-seven years, generated annual revenue of approximately $20 million. The success has not come with any particular formula regarding the ratio of news and advertising content, just the opposite in fact. The amount of space devoted to what is called the "news hole" is determined by the news itself, the editors said. Table 4 shows the growth of *The Chronicle*, in overall pages, from 1966 through 1993.

TABLE 4
TOTAL PAGE COUNTS FOR ISSUES, 1966-1993

Issue	Pages	Issue	Pages
November 23, 1966	8	September 15, 1980	56
September 13, 1967	12	September 16, 1981	56
September 23, 1968	8	September 15, 1982	72
September 15, 1969	12	September 14, 1983	64
September 28, 1970	12	September 12, 1984	72
September 27, 1971	12	September 18, 1985	80
September 25, 1972	16	September 17, 1986	88
September 10, 1973	16	September 16, 1987	96*
September 16, 1974	24	September 14, 1988	96*
September 15, 1975	32	September 13, 1989	108*
September 13, 1976	32	September 12, 1990	104*
September 12, 1977	32	September 18, 1991	96*
September 11, 1978	48	September 16, 1992	96*
September 17, 1979	64	September 15, 1993	96*

Source: *The Chronicle of Higher Education.*

Note: *Two sections. After the premier issue, the issue dated closest to September 15 was used for the comparison.

The Chronicle's success has not been without its fits and starts. Gwaltney, known for his expansive delegation of responsibility to staff members and a continued willingness to risk, has also demonstrated the flexibility to eat his own words. "I've done it often and have found that it doesn't really cause indigestion" (Gwaltney, 1992c). At times, the editor/owner has had to eat more than words.

Spinoffs and Other Experiments

The same year *The Chronicle* became independent, Gwaltney began looking to expand the four-year-old *Chronicle Review* to audiences beyond campuses. The culturally oriented section had begun with just a few book reviews, then included reviews of magazines and journals, eventually movie reviews, and an occasional opinion piece. In September 1978, the *Review* became a pull-out section with its own staff and its own advertising. Gwaltney wanted to combine reviews of serious books with approachable graphics and writing.

Soon, it became obvious that a new publication was in the making, and the *Review* section metamorphosed into *Books & Arts*. The generous white space, dashing type, and exquisite use of photography and art that distinguished the publication later made the tabloid a finalist in the National Magazine Award graphics category. *Books & Arts* adopted a cover design featuring a three-column photo similar to the design *The Chronicle* assumed in the summer of 1992. Cover subjects were drawn from every aspect of cultural endeavor and included author Tom Wolfe (September 14, 1979), actor James Earl Jones (September 28, 1979), entertainer Bette Midler (October 12, 1979), cellist Nathaniel Rosen (November 9, 1979), jazz pianist and composer Mary Lou Williams (December 7, 1979) and, trumpeter Dizzy Gillespie (January 25, 1980), among others.

Books & Arts was the epitome of the magazine Gwaltney always wanted. He targeted the publication to a general circulation audience, with professors forming only the core of the group. The publication was sent free of charge to *The Chronicle*'s subscribers for a year. As subscriptions expired, subscribers were pitched to buy both publications. About twenty percent to twenty-five percent did just that. The response represented a high conversion rate for any publishing endeavor, but it was not substantial enough to meet Gwaltney's aggressively optimistic financial planning.

With a great sense of trauma, he suspended publication of *Books & Arts* in early 1980 after less than six months, because the spinoff was losing money at the rate of $1 million a year. Ten staff members, including Ted Weidlein, were laid off, with Weidlein to return about six months later.

"We were just too dumb about the realities of general circulation publications," Gwaltney assessed the venture. "We learned how not to do a lot of things, such as national advertising and circulation on a national scale" (1992e).

The passage of more than a decade has not lessened Gwaltney's fondness for the venture. He continues to weigh a *Books & Arts* revival, vowing a greater sophistication on the business side the next time around. In the meantime, the *Scholarship* and *Publishing* sections have filled the void by focusing on scholarly publishing, books, and campus research.

In more recent years, Gwaltney's entrepreneurial urges and investment strategy have been targeted at *The Chronicle of Philanthropy*, launched in October 1988, which reached the black side of the ledger sheet several months before its fifth birthday. The publication evolved from general coverage of philanthropy, which was added to *The Chronicle* as a section in the early 1980s. As the subject was covered more in-depth, the editors noticed the growing amount of space devoted to corporate philanthropy.

In the fall of 1987, after ten years as managing editor of *The Chronicle*, Phil Semas took a leave of absence from the day-to-day newspaper operation to research a publication in the field of philanthropy. His information gathering process uncovered a statistic: the United States has some 450,000 501(c)(3) non-profit organizations. He determined that about 100,000 of these 501(c)(3) groups are big enough to be considered potential subscribers. These were the non-profit groups with income of at least $25,000 a year and required to file a tax return. "I spent the first two or three months talking to people," Semas said. "I decided there was a market and advertising potential" (Semas, 1992c).

Gwaltney encouraged Semas to write a promotion letter to describe the editorial product. With that, they conducted a test-market promotion. The results, Semas remembered, were mixed—not bad enough to scrap the project; not good enough to feel overly confident. Results were further analyzed; budgets formulated. In May 1988, Gwaltney, Crowl, and Semas decided to proceed with *The Chronicle of Philanthropy*. After five years, the biweekly newspaper, formatted similarly to *The Chronicle*, boasted a staff of fifteen editorial people and shared business resources, such as accounting and advertising sales, with *The Chronicle*. Circulation had risen from an initial 10,000 to 30,066, with a pass-along rate of 3.3 readers per copy. Table 5 shows the steady growth of *The Chronicle of Philanthropy* in its first five years.

TABLE 5
THE CHRONICLE OF PHILANTHROPY'S
SIX-MONTH AVERAGE PAID CIRCULATION, 1989-1993

Date	Circulation	Date	Circulation
December 1989	16,112	June 1990	8,523
December 1990	20,931	June 1991	22,970
December 1991	24,881	June 1992	27,097
December 1992	28,785	June 1993	30,066

Source: The Audit Bureau of Circulations.

Gwaltney continues the experimenting on all fronts. The February 24, 1993, issue introduced *Notes from Academe*, a dilettantish column, whose only subject matter limitation is an association with higher education. In April 1993, *The Chronicle* launched a service on the Internet, the network of technology networks that enables computer users worldwide to communicate with one another. First month connections to *The Chronicle*'s listing service, called *Academe This Week*, totaled nearly forty thousand. Producers prowled the paper's West End Washington offices during the fall of 1993, in preparation for the newspaper's first promotional video. And staffers know that a rainy weekend likely will bring editor Gwaltney into the office on Monday with a list of new ideas.

CHAPTER IV

EARNING A REPUTATION: THE NEWSGATHERING PROCESS

Between the Bylines

Robert Jacobson had spent three days at the Holiday Inn in Denver, monitoring the news in late May 1989, as student protests exploded into mass uprisings in China. The protests had the endorsements of at least seven Chinese university presidents and the heads of several research institutes. On May 16, hundreds of Chinese intellectuals, including an estimated five hundred faculty members at Beijing University, had signed a public statement of support for the movement. The statement, issued during Soviet President Mikhail Gorbachev's state visit to China, came on the twenty-third anniversary of the Chinese Communist Party's issuance of the "May 16 Circular," which contained the basic plan for China's Cultural Revolution under Mao Zedong (Chinese intellectuals', 1989, p. A29). By Friday, May 26, tens of thousands of pro-democracy students occupied Tiananmen Square, the symbolic center of Chinese power. A letter from the top military command had been printed in every newspaper, urging soldiers to obey commands to impose martial law (Branson, 1989, p. A27).

Jacobson, *The Chronicle*'s international editor at the time, could have already been in the mainland Asian country, but he had stretched his departure from Washington with this stopover to carefully consider the final departure decision. Ultimately, he would depart May 24.

Jacobson had planned this trip, his second to China, in April. The first had been in the fall of 1987 when he visited fifteen universities in six Chinese cities. The timing of this return trip, coincidental to the student unrest, now promised stories neither he nor his editors had envisioned. They also knew that such stories, angled especially for *The Chronicle*, would not be forthcoming from wire services. But they acknowledged the danger in the assignment. They could not, of course, foresee the violent end to the protests.

The telephone in Jacobson's Denver hotel room rang. Gwaltney and Scully were both on the line. "We don't want you to go," Gwaltney said. The statement could have been an order. Jacobson pleaded for the chance to make the final decision about the trip.

"To their credit," he later said of the editors (Jacobson, 1993), "they let me make the call. I went, and I never regretted it."

One of the last foreigners allowed into the country, Jacobson was at Beijing University when the government made its bloody June 4, 1989, assault on the students. Along with Chinese students, he listened to eyewitnesses who returned from the site of the slaughter; and he heard a tape recording made at the massacre scene. He talked to students and faculty members about the distress in China's academic world that may have led to the brutal crackdown and then the seeming end to hopes for campus freedoms. Jacobson wrote, "After the massacre, all bets were off about the future of Chinese universities, let alone the rest of Chinese society" (Jacobson, 1989, p. A34).

Back at home, *The Chronicle*'s reporters covered the solidarity marches of Chinese students in the United States, efforts to get aid and information to China, the disrupted travel plans of faculty and students, and the fate of student exchange programs. *The Chronicle* published questions and answers, provided by the National Association for Foreign Student Affairs, about new United States visa policies for Chinese citizens at American colleges and universities (Answers, 1989, p. A31).

The Chronicle's coverage of the Tiananmen Square incident and related campus issues provided readers a dramatic example of the newspaper's newsgathering prowess. Other examples of the publication's dedication to delivering the news perhaps are taken for granted by the typical reader, but, within the newsroom, extraordinary reporting efforts regularly contribute to an internal *esprit de corps*. Such a situation occurred after the normal Thursday deadline for the March 16, 1988, issue.

Word came to *The Chronicle* newsroom that the newly appointed president of Gallaudet University had resigned. Earlier that week, the appointment of Elisabeth A. Zinser, a hearing person, as the seventh president of the nation's only university for the deaf had prompted bitter student protests (DeLoughry, 1988, p. A1). *The Chronicle* had a report and a photograph of the protests. Zinser's resignation, however, represented a major development in the ongoing story. Gwaltney decided to tear up the front page and include coverage of the presidential resignation. The story was updated, and the newspaper was printed—almost on time.

As a weekly, *The Chronicle* combined its mission to deliver news with the challenge of providing perspective. The result is called "synthesis reporting" at *The Chronicle*, a journalistic approach that the newspaper's editors identify as one of the publication's editorial strengths.

Synthesis Reporting

Managing editor Malcolm Scully (1992k) defined synthesis reporting as a "journalism of ideas," or a discussion of ideas as well as the reporting of events. As *The Chronicle* grew in staff and expertise, the in-depth synthesis journalism pieces became more frequent. The publication became dotted with its signature, arrow-like bullets used to highlight a summary list of points covered by a report or other listings of data.

The reporting strategy resulted in pieces such as the March 16, 1970, front-page review of the United States' lack of scholarly competence on Vietnam. Two months before the killings at Kent State

University, *The Chronicle* pointed out that the country had not a single Vietnam scholar who:

1. held a full professorship;
2. had substantial standing in his discipline;
3. had a language background in Vietnamese, French, and Chinese;
4. had conducted in-country field research; and,
5. had a body of published work dealing with Vietnam (Jones, 1970a, p. 1).

Assistant editor William Hamilton Jones cited a variety of interrelated reasons for the dearth of Vietnamese scholars in the United States.

First, he wrote, there had been little academic tradition. Because the United States had had few missionary, trading, or colonial contacts with Southeast Asia, American scholars had never had a basis for becoming interested in Vietnam the way they had in China or Korea. Jones characterized the commitment necessary to become a Vietnam scholar as "prohibitive for many people. Mastery of language alone is likely to take five to seven years of intensive work, since fluency in Vietnamese and French, as well as in Chinese, is required for anyone concerned with historical questions" (Jones, 1970a, p. 4). *The Chronicle* writer also noted other problems.

He quoted David Marr, a Vietnam historian at Cornell University, about the lack of student interest in Vietnamese studies:

My own hypothesis is that many students today just don't belong in Vietnam in any way, shape, or form—even as scholars. Given the fact that a lot of students are alienated from the war, they want to avoid tangling themselves in the rat's nest. There's a feeling that it's a very loaded subject (Jones, 1970a, p. 5).

"Something like 'Black Professors on White Campuses' (Middleton, 1978, p. 1) was the kind of story we could do after we had grown a bit," remembered Semas (1992c), who was managing editor at the time the story was published. The article was an insightful look at the fact that many black professors, despite certain campus progress, still felt isolated and uncertain of their futures in academe. Assistant news editor Lorenzo Middleton's article identified tenure as the major concern among young black and other minority-group faculty members on white campuses. He wrote:

> Some have become discouraged by the pressures of working in white institutions and voluntarily have gone to black colleges or left higher education altogether. But many are part of what James E. Blackwell, a sociologist at the University of Massachusetts in Boston, calls a 'whole generation of young minority faculty members who are moving from institution to institution because they did not get tenure at the institution where they were originally hired' (Middleton, 1978, p. 8).

Whatever the topic, *The Chronicle*'s synthesis approach brings academic readers the weekly reassurance that they are not alone in various campus issues and experiences.

"It forecasts the future for people in the middle (of the country). There's no question about that," said Shirley Chater (1993), who was president of Texas Woman's University in Denton, Texas, until fall, 1993, when she was confirmed as commissioner of the Social Security Administration for the Clinton Administration. "I read what happens on the two coasts, and I know perfectly well what is going to happen in Texas six months later."

Texas Woman's pays for a subscription to *The Chronicle* for each of its regents to provide some understanding and perspective of the overall U.S. higher education system in order for them to have a context for viewing their own university. The University of North Carolina System, too, buys the newspaper for its regents. William C. Friday (1993), president emeritus, called the newspaper the "only consistent voice higher education has in interpreting our work to the country."

Friday also cited *The Chronicle* as the only news publication that took the "time and money" to thoroughly interpret the nearly twelve-year battle, what many called the "great desegregation war," between the University of North Carolina and the Department of Health, Education and Welfare. At issue was the university's desegregation plan for its multi-campus system, which included both predominantly white and black institutions (Friday, 1993).

Friday said *The Chronicle* interpreted the struggle correctly as one of "academic control," while the mass media reported allegations and counter-allegations and cast the situation as a racial debate. Even when the dispute was settled in June 1981, the *New York Times* followed its news report with an editorial that expressed doubt as to whether the government and the university had found a "satisfactory path" (North Carolina's College Deal, 1981). CBS aired a *Sunday Morning* segment that Friday said gave the false impression that North Carolina had done almost nothing to integrate its sixteen-campus university system before the settlement. The university president complained to the network, which responded with a story the following Sunday that included a lengthy interview with Friday (North Carolina President, 1981).

"To sum up, if higher education has a consistent and interpretive voice, it is *The Chronicle of Higher Education.* I've never heard an allegation of bias," Friday said (1993). "If we didn't have it, it would have to be invented."

Six-point Success

Agate type, measured as "6-point" in the trade, sells newspapers. To Gwaltney, *The Chronicle*'s extensive agate type listings, more than any single feature, make the newspaper indispensable to its campus-bound readers. In formulating editorial content, the editor understood that university administrators and faculty, especially, often feel isolated on their campuses. What sustains them is a feeling of community—mostly gained through meetings and scholarly publications—that someone, somewhere, shares their interest.

Early in *The Chronicle*'s history, Gwaltney capitalized on this need for an essence of "community." Twice a year, he began publishing pull-out calendar sections. Later came the semi-annual publication of *Events in Academe*, which includes information about meetings and convention sites, and the annual *Almanac*, which includes a variety of facts and statistics concerning higher education and related political, social, and economic topics.

These supplements complement the emphasis on agate-sized listings, often published under the heading "Fact File," and bold-faced names found within the newspaper since its earliest issues. Gwaltney noted many lists in early issues that he had typed himself. No other higher education-oriented publication compares with *The Chronicle* in terms of numbers of appointments, resignations, deaths, events, deadlines, and other listings (Gwaltney, 1992e).

In addition, *The Chronicle* has served as the newspaper of record for such statistics as the annual salary survey conducted by the American Association of University Professors and the administrator salary survey conducted by the College and University Personnel Association. The newspaper annually publishes the list and survey of the National Collegiate Athletic Association's resolutions. One of its earliest published and longest running such statistical reference is the Department of Education's tabulations of the distribution by race of student bodies at thousands of institutions.

Increased sophistication in computer technology and data-base management led *The Chronicle* in 1992 to appoint Douglas Lederman as special projects editor to head development of its own statistical listings. The effort's first project, a listing of campus crime statistics, was published January 20, 1993. The project was *The Chronicle*'s response to a federal law, effective September 1, 1992, that required campuses to publish crime statistics. In addition to the raw data from 2,400 schools, the newspaper published a series of stories about how the law was implemented and how institutions were responding to it.

As *The Chronicle* has become more aggressive in its reporting, its constituency has become more aware of what the publication's editors are quick to point out: the preposition in the publication's name has significance. The newspaper is *The Chronicle OF Higher Education*, not *FOR*. At times, the subtle language distinction causes not-so-subtle contention among readers who expect more institutional cheerleading.

Power, Pomp, and Circumstance

The newspaper followed its crime statistics project by gathering salary data from federal tax forms filed with the Internal Revenue Service by private universities. The resulting list of the top executive's compensation, as well as that of the five highest-paid staff members, at 190 institutions was published May 5, 1993. Accompanying the survey and its explanatory reviews was another article that provided readers a rare look inside *The Chronicle*'s newsgathering process—and the fact that, six years after a law first required nonprofit institutions to make public their primary federal tax form, requests for the information "still make many college officials squirm. Others get downright hostile" (Lederman, 1993b, p. A14).

Special projects editor Lederman explained in the article that the newspaper had asked 190 private colleges, selected according to their classifications by the Carnegie Foundation for the Advancement of Teaching, for a copy of their tax forms. Most exceeded their legal obligations, Lederman reported, by mailing a copy of the Form 990. Some colleges followed the letter of the law and required *The Chronicle*'s reporter to visit their campuses to view the information in person. Others violated IRS rules by omitting parts of the tax form or by requiring reporters to say why they wanted to see the information. One institution, Lederman reported, refused to let a reporter even see the form in person. *The Chronicle* subsequently obtained the college's Form 990 from the Internal Revenue Service, leaving the federal agency to deal with the college's alleged violation.

Publication of the survey, which showed presidents' pay ranging from $1 to $395,725, brought immediate and heated criticism. In a lengthy letter to the editor in the June 2, 1993, issue (Merkowitz, 1993, p. B4), the director of public affairs for the American Council on Education took *The Chronicle* to task for "a distorted picture of executive pay scale in higher education." The Council's David Merkowitz contended that the survey sample was skewed toward the largest and/or wealthiest schools, and, thus, was not representative of higher education in general. The letter concluded:

At a time when higher education is under attack from numerous quarters, and when the public is justifiably concerned about issues of access and cost, you owe your readers a more complete, contextual presentation of such data, together with a more thoughtful exploration of the factors that affect executive compensation (Merkowitz, 1993, p. B4).

Higher education consultant Allan Ostar, former president of the American Association of State Colleges and Universities, was also critical, calling the publication of the salary survey an "unfair shot" and "gotcha journalism" (Ostar, 1993). At the same time, however, he acknowledged that if *The Chronicle* tried to be a cheerleader, its integrity would be undercut.

Gwaltney remained unfazed by the criticism. And why not. About seventy-five daily and weekly newspapers across the country picked up and printed all or parts of the chief executive salary information. "At public institutions, virtually everything is up for public inspection. And that extends to private universities on the basis of tax exemption. If they expect an exemption from taxes, they have to reveal things like salaries if the government requires it. So be it" (Gwaltney, 1993j).

Indeed, sacred cows are an extinct breed at *The Chronicle*, a fact to which Robert Atwell, president of the American Council on Education, would have readily attested in early 1992. Atwell, who heads higher education's most powerful advocacy group in Washington and whose name appears as a frequent source for *The Chronicle*'s reporters, found himself and his organization accused of racism and hostility toward black colleges in a front-page article in the newspaper (Jaschik, 1992, p. A1). The president of the National Association for Equal Opportunity in Higher Education, a major lobbying group for historically black colleges, had made the charge in a letter sent to the presidents of black colleges and obtained by *The Chronicle*.

"It was a big tempest," Atwell reflected (1993). "They (*The Chronicle*) had to cover that in a major way. I was the accused, as it were, and yet I felt that everything they did was completely fair."

What *The Chronicle* did was allow Atwell to respond in the fourth paragraph (Jaschik, 1992, p. A1), before the article jumped inside the newspaper to page A37. Atwell was quoted as being "saddened and angered" by the letter, which he said was inaccurate in its descriptions of the Council. The newspaper also cited three black college presidents by name who thought Atwell had been supportive of their institutions and several others who "did not want to be identified because they did not want to disagree publicly" with the head of their institutional lobbying effort (Jaschik, 1992, p. A37). A follow-up article, which also ran on the front page, appeared a week later (Black-college, 1992, A1) to report that a "summit" meeting of black college presidents was being planned to "establish new priorities and positions" for dealing with the federal government. Later the same month, two letters to the editor expressed support for each side of the controversy (Lecca, 1992 and Thomas, 1992).

The Atwell situation illustrated *The Chronicle*'s reasoning against its pursuing advocacy journalism. Instead of being pushed to take a stance and express an editorial opinion, the newspaper presented both sides of a complicated and politically sensitive issue. Reader letters, too, were able to express varying viewpoints.

Even Atwell, who might have courted the newspaper's favor, characterized the newspaper's no-editorial policy as wise. "I think it would be kind of murderous for them to get into all the crazy fights in this business. I think they're dead right about that," he said (1993).

CHAPTER V

INSIDE THE IVORY TOWER: ISSUES IN HIGHER EDUCATION

Campus Unrest

The old school dance, prom dresses, and fraternity parties composed Hollywood's version of higher education until the mid-1960s. Then came the free speech movement, the civil rights movement, and the Vietnam War protests. President Richard Nixon's decision to send U.S. troops into Cambodia and the Kent State University killings heightened the turmoil on American college campuses. Stephen R. Graubard, editor of *Daedalus, the Journal of the American Academy of Arts & Sciences*, wrote, "The university has, with even greater intensity, become the focus of the nation's tensions, and many issues which formerly seemed the parochial concern of the academic community have suddenly assumed much wider significance" (Graubard, 1970, p. v).

"Campus unrest was a tremendous story for us. And we reacted to the disasters. We went to Mississippi State, Cornell, Yale," Gwaltney said (1992g). "What we were doing is what the daily press calls a second-day story—in-depth kinds of coverage that gained in credibility because of the perspective. We were doing more than the war correspondent kind of reporting."

The Chronicle's small staff seemed to stretch itself to be everywhere at once. The same front page that reported the Kent State shootings, on May 11, 1970, also presented a minute-by-minute "diary" account of an anxious night at the Yale University "command post" during a massive demonstration in support of Bobby Seale and other Black Panthers awaiting trial on murder charges. Assistant editor William Hamilton Jones described in detail the extensive preparations made by the Yale administration to assure, in President Kingman Brewster, Jr.'s words, a "peaceful and non-violent" weekend (Jones, 1970b, p. 1). He wrote:

> Special telephone lines were installed, including direct lines connecting Mr. Chauncey (assistant to the president) to the chief of the New Haven police and the chief of the campus police. In addition, telephones were installed for a twenty-four-hour-a-day information service, where people could call to verify rumors or find answers to their questions (Jones, 1970b, p. 1).

Longtime staffers have vivid memories of those days. Weidlein recalled the day he was sitting in the newsroom and was asked by Gwaltney and Miller to take the next plane to New Orleans and then drive to Baton Rouge, where two students at Southern University had just been killed during a protest (Weidlein, 1993i). Scully said that for one month in 1968, he and Semas were on the road so much that the only time they saw each other was during a chance passing at the Baltimore-Washington International Airport (1993i). If the staffers were not back in Washington by deadline in those days before Federal Express, facsimile machines, and modems, they would telephone the office and dictate stories.

The reporting efforts led to such coverage as the May 19, 1969, package of stories and photographs. The front page of *The Chronicle* carried under its masthead four dramatic photographs illustrating the headline, "Violent Spring." At Voorhees College in South Carolina, one of thirty students occupying the administration building was shown, rifle by her side, keeping a vigil at a window. At Columbia University, a student ripped down a red flag from the roof of a radical-occupied building. At the University of Wisconsin, a bicycle-riding student is pictured being subdued by Madison policemen during a campus demonstration. At Dartmouth College, a state policeman restrained one of about fifty-five students evicted from the administration building.

Below the photographs, a banner headline, reading "How 3 Constituent Groups See Student Aims," served as an umbrella for the three subheadings: "Faculty," "Alumni," and "Students." Also on the page, an article labeled "Analysis" pointed out that when the Students for a Democratic Society emerged with their faces covered after a one-day occupation of the mathematics and Fayerweather buildings at Columbia University that spring, the event had marked "the end of a period in the development of the New Left."

"What we managed to do was to explain points of view in ways I don't think a lot of people had heard before," Scully said. "Phil (Semas) had a lot of contacts within the student movement and by treating them, reporting on them, the same way we treated and reported on administrators, we became a natural vehicle for providing information a lot of people did not have" (Scully, 1992g).

Indeed, Semas, who started working for *The Chronicle* in 1968 as its West Coast stringer, or correspondent, was a natural selection for such assignments, thanks to a previous stint at College Press Service, a news service for student newspapers.

"Students could recognize Phil as a kindred soul," Gwaltney said, jokingly (1992g). In other words, Semas translated for his boss, he looked like a campus radical. Semas was once introduced by a protestor to another protestor: "This guy's from *The Chronicle of Higher Education*. It's a newspaper for college administrators, but it doesn't pander to its readers" (Semas, 1992a).

The reputation gave the publication access to sources, such as university presidents, who might not have made themselves as accessible to other newspapers. Throughout its history, *The Chronicle* has relied on its access to key people in higher education to produce more insightful coverage with fewer resources.

"Over the years, people have learned to trust us, even though we don't always write what they like." Gwaltney said (1992g). "But they trust us to treat them fairly."

The Chronicle even managed occasionally to insert a relieving tone of humor amid crisis. On April 22, 1974, above a front-page photograph of students protesting the arrest of more than fifty persons on drug charges and clashing with police at the University of Maryland, the publication simply noted: "It Must Be Spring."

After the investigation of the Kent State killings, the Scranton Commission on Campus Unrest compiled all the photographs it could obtain, including those taken by the media and others. *The Chronicle* ran fifty-seven photos (Sequence, 1970), an inch-and-a-half deep each and four across the page, in an effort to reconstruct the events of the day—who fired the first shot, who was there, why they shot. And, when the Scranton Commission issued its report, *The Chronicle*, anticipating bureaucratic government delays in its dissemination, published the document's full text in its October 5, 1970, issue.

Despite the magnitude of campus unrest stories, this coverage was not the only area upon which *The Chronicle* built its editorial reputation. Gwaltney likened the situation to that of the *New York Times* or the *Washington Post* the day after the bombing of Pearl Harbor. There was other news to be reported.

Civil Rights

Racial unrest coincided, or perhaps collided, with the campus war protests of the 1960s. The death of Martin Luther King, Jr. in the spring of 1968 pushed the activists not only into the streets but also brought calls for changes into the classrooms. Many colleges and universities took steps toward improving the status, and numbers, of black students.

New York University was one of many universities that canceled classes after the death of Dr. King and called for "deliberations by students, faculty members, and administrators to design programs to eradicate the injustice of racism in the university and in the United States," *The Chronicle* reported (Brann, 1968). It announced new initiatives in its recruitment of non-white students, faculty members, and administrators. In addition, the university set up a Martin Luther King, Jr. scholarship fund with a goal of raising $1 million. The university also took actions to strengthen remedial programs and to establish new courses in African and Afro-American history, art, and literature.

Still, violence continued. The front page of the December 2, 1968, issue of *The Chronicle* carried a photograph of San Francisco State College's acting president, S. I. Hayakawa, disconnecting wires on a sound truck used by student demonstrators who had refused to hear him speak. Racial violence had kept the university closed for nearly a month and had resulted in the resignation of Robert R. Smith as the college's president. Smith predicted, at the time, that "the same kind of crisis" would be facing many urban colleges and universities (Semas, 1968, p.1). Smith attributed the crisis to the result of "rising aspirations for educational opportunity, particularly among minority groups who have previously had less than an equal opportunity for higher education."

Smith's words were accurate. Whereas the Vietnam War ended, civil rights issues have continued. As the issues became more complicated, *The Chronicle*'s coverage became more comprehensive. An example is found in the publication's handling of the July 1992, Supreme Court ruling in a Mississippi case that specified, for the first time, how states must show they have removed the vestiges of past segregation. Labeled "A New Era for Desegregation," the coverage in the July 8, 1992, issue of *The Chronicle* included a complete text of the *United States v. Fordice* opinions, an explanation, and analysis of the ruling as well as a look at two campuses in Mississippi that the justices suggested be merged.

"The battles of the '60s were relatively simple," Scully explained. "You knew who the good guys were and who the bad guys were. There were laws on the books that needed to be changed. With hindsight, these were easy victories." The more difficult issues to cover, he added, included the fate of historically black colleges, the shift of racial balances, the increase of Hispanics and Asian-Americans on campuses. Civil rights shifted from black issues to ethnic issues. The new buzzword: multiculturalism.

Multiculturalism

Gwaltney identified multiculturalism as one of the great American stories, in addition to being a higher education story, to be reported in the 1990s. "What is happening to this country can be either dismaying to you or exciting to you and marvelously edifying depending upon where you sit," the editor said (Gwaltney, 1992k). "I find it one of the most exciting periods societally."

The term multiculturalism quickly became linked to "political correctness," a phrase so all pervasive that its initials, "P.C.," are quite sufficient identification on any college or university campus. Neither term appeared in *The Chronicle*'s indexes until Volume XXXVII, for the period September 5, 1990, through August 14, 1991, the same academic year that Dinesh D'Souza's book, *Illiberal Education: The Politics of Race and Sex on Campus*, helped bring political correctness and multiculturalism to the attention of the mass media.

Campus debate was further fueled by such instances as a University of Texas at Austin professor's contention that he was replaced as head of the English department's honors program because he criticized a proposed multiculturalism requirement. The day before he was informed that he was to be replaced, James Duban had spoken out at a University Council meeting against a proposal that would have required all undergraduates to take courses in minority and Third World studies (Mangan, 1991, p. A15).

Of course, much earlier cultural sensitivities can be found in *The Chronicle*'s evolution of terminology. The word "Negro" was used until the summer of 1969 when "black" became the preference. Later that fall, *The Chronicle* took a hard look at demands for black studies that went far beyond the mere addition of a few courses in history and culture (Crowl, p. 4). And a major article, headlined "The State of Black Studies" in December 1975, reported that "black studies programs are not where they thought they would be by this time, but they're slowly becoming more established" (Winkler, p. 5). A photography feature in January 1978, covered the curriculum activities of Navajo Community College in Arizona, an institution attempting to satisfy the cultural needs of its American Indian students while compensating for their poor educational background (Phillips, p. 10).

In more recent years, Hispanics and Asian-Americans have received increasing coverage in *The Chronicle*'s pages as the ethnic groups' representations have grown not only on campuses but in the general population. For example, a portrait of Antonio Rigual, the founder of the Hispanic Association of Colleges and Universities in San Antonio, Texas, discussed activities being undertaken to support Hispanics before, during, and after the college years (Mangan, 1990, p. A3). A "minority issues committee," comprising several of the newspaper's reporters and editors, meets regularly to review the publication's coverage.

Women in Higher Education

Within the kaleidoscope of minority issues and equal rights, women have struggled to define gender-specific issues. Campuses have served as incubators for much of the discussion affecting society at large. Women, after all, outperform men in high school and college. They get higher grades on average, are awarded more scholarships, and complete bachelor's degrees at a faster pace than men, according to federal research published in 1991 (Stipp, 1992, p. B8). After college, however, they tend to receive lower average pay, encounter slower advancement, and experience more unemployment than men. In higher education, as in society, women often assume the roles they have come to expect. *The Chronicle*'s managing editor Scully remembered a Midwest meeting of radical faculty members. The women looked around and realized they had assumed the same roles within the radical faculty group that they had in traditional systems.

"The same thing happened to black women involved in civil rights issues," he said (Scully, 1992h). "Our coverage evolved because we began to hear what the women players were saying." Of course, these were the early voices of affirmative action and were echoes of the complaints filed with the Department of Labor in January 1970, by the Women's Equity Action League, a group asking that court action be taken against colleges and universities found discriminating against women (Scully, 1970, p. 3).

In one of its first major reports on women in higher education in 1970 (Scully, p. 2), *The Chronicle* ran a photograph of a woman in a university lab in 1919. The cutline, or the identification for the photograph, further made the point: "Many people argue that conditions for women in higher education have improved little since 1919, when this picture was taken." The report pointed to National Education Association statistics that showed the median nine-month salary for women in higher education was $7,732 for 1965–1966, 16.6 percent less than the $9,275 median for men. In the same piece, *The Chronicle* discussed the discrepancies between the numbers of female and male Ph.D.'s. The article addressed sexual harassment, the influence of changing values, and other documented discrimination and difficulties for academic women.

More than twenty years after that early report, Scully assessed (1992h), "Women are by no means at the end of the tunnel in terms of getting an equal role in higher education." He pointed to the increasing sophistication of such coverage in *The Chronicle*, however, including an increasing emphasis on the role of women in scholarship.

For example, a December 1992, issue featured the work of Annette B. Weiner, an anthropologist who radically changed the way ethnographers approach fieldwork (McMillen, p. A6). Weiner came across her field of expertise quite by accident, *The Chronicle* article explained. As a graduate student, she had gone to the Trobriand Islands of Papua New Guinea to study the art and economics of the wood carvings that are made by male villagers and sold to tourists. Along the way, two women approached her and took her to a ceremony in another village. There, women were taking bundles of banana leaves and throwing them on the ground, calling out someone's name. The women told Weiner the bundles were just like money. The ceremony, she learned, was called *sagali* and represented the distribution of women's wealth to commemorate someone's death. Weiner went on to study how the ceremony related to larger power relationships.

"If you look at our *Scholarship* section, every generation of scholars redefines its specialty," Gwaltney said (1992k). "We see over and over that where something we thought was settled is reopened and questioned. This will continue. There is no such thing as a generation. It is continual."

Athletics

In other words, *plus ca change, plus c'est la meme chose* ("The more things change, the more things stay the same"). The saying, coined by French novelist Alphonse Karr, once provided one of Gwaltney's favorite column subheadings in his hometown *Baltimore Sun*. The axiom also describes his sentiments while writing what seem to be repeating headlines.

Perhaps athletics, more than most areas within higher education, illustrates recurrent themes in higher education. In fact, the $2 million, forty-seven-page report, *Keeping Faith with the Student-Athlete: A New Model for Intercollegiate Athletics*, issued by the independent Knight Commission in March 1991, mentioned that a 1929 Carnegie report on intercollegiate athletics used much the same language (Maisel, 1991).

The Chronicle's headlines throughout the years have reflected common themes:

> Government Tells Colleges To End Bias in Sports (April 5, 1967)
> NCAA Regroups; Penalizes S. W. Louisiana (August 31, 1973)
> The NCAA Diagrams a New Play for Re-aligning College Sports (December 13, 1976)
> NCAA to Vote on Tougher Academic Rules for Athletes (December 15, 1980)
> NCAA Presidents Call New Meeting on Sports Reform (January 14, 1987)
> NCAA Overwhelmingly Backs Reform Plan; Coaching Staffs and Costs Will Be Cut (January 16, 1991)

Some of the above referenced headlines were written by Jack Crowl, who, by the early 1980s, was heading the publication's business operations as publisher. Crowl, who was managing editor from 1972 to 1978, could not, however, completely abandon the editorial side nor envision himself as a full-time business manager. So, he signed on as a headline writer. He rationalized that the activity would guarantee his knowing what was going on every week in the newspaper and that the task only required one day a week.

He started to notice an increasing number of stories about brewing scandals in college athletics. "It seemed to me that athletics had the potential of causing a great deal of harm, if nothing else, to what was going on at the rest of the university," he said (Crowl, 1993). "If we were really going to be *The Chronicle of Higher Education*, we should be covering how athletics intersects with the rest of the university."

Gwaltney agreed. So did other editors and writers. But no one stepped forward to assume the task. Crowl finally decided to undertake the assignment himself. He hired a reporter, and the two of them spent several months talking to people, gathering information, and reading. *The Chronicle*'s *Athletics* section made its debut September 1, 1982, with the lead article, "Colleges Urged to Teach Athletes, Coaches the Dangers of Drug Abuse and 'Doping'" (McDonald and Vance, 1982, p. 25). Assistant editor N. Scott Vance reported that thirty-five percent of 167 coaches, trainers, and physicians surveyed by a drug-education committee of the National Collegiate Athletic Association (NCAA) said steroids were "helpful" to athletic performance, and eight percent said amphetamines, or "uppers," were helpful. Seven of fifteen swimming coaches, eight of eighteen track coaches, eight of twenty-one basketball coaches, and thirteen of fifty-five football coaches called steroids helpful; twelve of thirty-seven trainers said they were helpful, and seven of twenty-three team physicians agreed (McDonald and Vance, 1982, p. 28).

Again, the timing proved right. College presidents, who had for years ignored involvement in athletics, started feeling pressure, from such diverse groups as faculty and Congress, to become active in instituting reforms. Rumblings went through the non-sports sectors of higher education about the way athletics were taking over and not necessarily playing by the same game rules as academic departments. Also to be considered was the growing financial clout of college sports. By 1986, college sports revenue had surpassed the $1 billion mark (Bedell, 1986, p. 20A).

In 1984, a Presidents Commission of chief executive officers from forty-four universities was formed within the National Collegiate Athletic Association. Within two years, the group pushed through three major changes, including a toughening of academic requirements for athletes, a strengthening of sanctions against NCAA rules violators, and a drug-testing program (Bedell, 1986, p 21A). William C. Friday, president emeritus of the University of North Carolina and co-chairman of the Knight Commission, credited *The Chronicle* with providing at least part of the impetus for the growing involvement of university presidents within the realm of athletics (Friday, 1993).

"The most important thing *The Chronicle of Higher Education* has done is regularly list all the institutions under [NCAA] sanctions," Friday said (1993). "The publication of that information has had a salutary effect. Presidents don't like to see their [institutions'] names on the list."

Gwaltney described the growth of athletics coverage as "more of a drumbeat than a single explosion" (1992i). The drumbeat continues its rhythm week after week as some issues are solved and others evolve. Sports are in many ways a microcosm of other issues on campuses. The area is often the place where matters of equity, ethics, and integration are dealt with quite publicly. Athletics is also an area which has both very compelling defenders and critics. It provides, Gwaltney added (1992i), "a lot of wonderful inconsistencies that make for good newspaper stuff."

In 1986, *The Chronicle* hired Doug Lederman, who initially supplemented Crowl's effort and eventually took over responsibility for the athletics coverage until late 1992 when he became special projects editor. Lederman, who brought a background in sports writing, said he was wary of taking *The Chronicle* post because he did not want to be labeled a "sports writer." His fears were unfounded. If anything, he became a curiosity among some of his sports writing colleagues; a trendsetter for others. He fielded more than his share of complaints about negative coverage. Instead of game coverage, *The Chronicle* has focused on policies and the intersection of sports and campus—a crossing point that often creates problems and, until recent years, was not a focus of mass media reporting.

The newspaper also has not hesitated to question the establishment. In its July 22, 1992, issue, *The Chronicle* produced its own survey about graduation statistics of black athletes that showed an NCAA study, by comparison, had "painted too rosy a picture" (Lederman, p. A31). *The Chronicle*'s piece presented a college-by-college breakdown of athlete graduation rates by race a month before the NCAA planned to release similar information in response to pressure from Congress.

"There's no question that a lot of universities have not put their sports programs into perspective," Lederman said (1992b). "Over the years, many universities have tried to use sports programs to help build their reputations. And, there is no question that the public cares more about sports than other parts of the university."

Gay Rights/AIDS

As a self-described reporter-driven newspaper, *The Chronicle,* over the years, has relied on reporters to raise its social, as well as editorial, consciousness. In the areas of gay rights and AIDS, the publication was well ahead of the mass media's coverage. While the mass media generally did not cover AIDS until the burst of publicity which accompanied the death of actor Rock Hudson in October 1985, boosted awareness, campus gay rights issues and mentions of AIDS can be found in *The Chronicle* as early as 1977 when such subjects were grouped under "Homosexuals" in the publication's index. In its index for Volume XIX (September 4, 1979 through February 25, 1980), *The Chronicle* cross-referenced the subject with the heading "Gay People (See Homosexuals)."

"We sent a reporter to the first two international meetings on AIDS, one in San Francisco, one in Stockholm," Scully said (1993a). "We recognized this was both a major research issue and a political issue."

The topic also elicited some of the most personally poignant reporting to appear in *The Chronicle*. In the December 4, 1985, issue, for example, writer Lawrence Biemiller chronicled the last weeks of an AIDS sufferer at the University of California at Berkeley from the point of view of the victim's lover. The story told of a Minnesota farm boy and a Mexican-American raised in Redwood City, California. The college dropouts decided to return to college together. The story graphically related the rapidity with which Paul, the twenty-seven-year-old AIDS victim, progressed through the disease's stages. The piece quoted Terry, his lover, "The problem for Paul was not how to fight the disease, but how to accept the notion of dying . . . The only question was how to die with grace and some sense of style" (Biemiller, 1985, p. 1).

AIDS coverage posed new verbiage standards for the media in general and *The Chronicle* in particular. "I'm the one who got the ultimate question because I was always the one who saw the copy last," Gwaltney said (1993a). "I did not anguish over the decisions very long. I had no problem using 'condom,' which was previously referred to in euphemistic terms. I feel you do a lot more harm by writing around things, by alluding to things, than if you go right out and say it within the bounds of accepted conventions."

Scully added (1993a), "One of our ground rules has been when you cannot explain what you're trying to explain to tell the story, without using the basic term, then use it. If it's extraneous, then don't."

Senior writer Biemiller, who in February, 1993, began writing the biweekly *Notes From Academe* column, said he has experienced no constraints on his writing. Of course, the *Notes* column, in particular, was created to be dilettantish and viscerally personal, and Biemiller acknowledged the writing is somewhat atypical of *The Chronicle*'s usual fare.

The story of the Berkeley AIDS sufferer opened with a vivid description of his lover's remembering the victim's insistence that horses were running loose in the bathroom of their home (Biemiller, 1985, p. 1). In one of his earliest *Notes* columns, Biemiller's description of a senior lecturer in music at the University of California at Los Angeles—"who's about as far out of the closet as a homosexual can get without wearing a tiara to work"—went untouched by an editor's computer key (Biemiller, 1993a, p. A51).

CHAPTER VI

BEYOND THE IVORY TOWER: OF ISSUES AND IMPORT

Progress or Retrogression?

"Currents and cross-currents; progress and retrogression; puzzles and paradoxes: all are found in higher education's 'Big Issues' of today. The promises of birth and the agonies of death can be found, too: new colleges, new curricula, new subject-matter—and dying colleges, dying curricula, dying subject-matter. And opportunity—for him who can recognize it, assess its meaning, accept its challenge" (Gwaltney, 1966a, p. 4).

Editor Gwaltney gave this survey of the landscape of higher education issues in July 1966, nearly five months prior to *The Chronicle*'s launch, in a speech at the national conference of the American Alumni Council. Although he ceased giving speeches in the early 1980s (citing time constraints and personal preference), he could likely revive many of his early talks to describe the evolution of issues in higher education. Instead, he has yielded to *The Chronicle*'s pages to unfold the currents and cross-currents, progress and retrogression, puzzles and paradoxes.

As the newspaper devoted editorial coverage to women's efforts toward gender-equity, the publication, too, reported Supreme Court Justice Sandra Day O'Connor's majority opinion, in a five-to-four vote, that the admissions policy of the nursing school at the Mississippi University for Women violated the equal-protection clause of the Constitution by discriminating against men (McDonald, 1982, p. 1).

The decades of *The Chronicle*'s coverage have documented the ebb and flow of campus administrative scandals. In one of the earliest to be reported by the newspaper, fourteen of the most aggressive and most successful college investment funds were caught in the middle of an insurance scandal involving the Equity Funding Corp., a one-time Wall Street glamour stock (Rein, 1973, p. 1). Slightly more than a year later, a science scandal shook Memorial Sloan-Kettering Cancer Center when a researcher was accused by a group of his colleagues of falsifying the results of skin-graft experiments on mice (Boffey, 1974, p. 7). A more recent controversy that filled many pages in *The Chronicle* centered on Stanford University's billing the government for questionable and improper overhead charges. The yearlong scandal culminated when Donald Kennedy announced, at the beginning of the 1991 fall term, his resignation as the institution's president (Grassmuck, 1991, p. A1).

New Issues and Dialogue

Long ago Gwaltney stopped worrying about filling *The Chronicle*'s pages. Recent decades have brought new issues for higher education as well as the resurfacing of past issues. There are also continuing changes and new political challenges in Washington that *The Chronicle* must interpret and put in perspective for its readership. The changes in academe and its related issues obviously reflect the broader shifts of societal norms. *The Chronicle*'s editors cited multiculturalism, the leadership of universities, funding, collegiality, the corporatization of higher education, faculty bashing, national service, and rising college costs among stories requiring continued coverage. *The Chronicle* strives to reflect the increasing complexity of such issues both in its news coverage and in its opinion pieces. "An increasing sophistication in coverage is being demanded," managing editor Scully said (1992g). "What's happening now is that the issues have become much more subtle."

Such delicate issues, for example, involve the future of historically black colleges and, in general, the shift of civil rights issues to broader ethnic issues. The latest issues for campus leaders, of course, reflect societal shifts. The impact of Asian-Americans and Hispanics on campuses in California follows the changing population of that state. Also, there was a time when it would have been unthinkable to link higher education with such concepts as antitrust. In recent years, however, antitrust allegations in regard to student aid have been leveled at institutions of higher education. And parents have been shocked when universities told them they no longer were going to act as substitute parents and monitor the comings and goings of their offspring.

Managing editor Scully suggested, "All these things add up to the major issue: an image problem. There's an impression that higher education hasn't done its job very well. Educators are having a hard time making a case. The bloom is off the rose."

As its image changes—sometimes being refined, sometimes damaged—higher education has become more and more like a service industry. *The Chronicle*'s editors suggested that higher education's image has changed as the area has become a huge business. That larger story, of course, has been composed of many smaller pieces. A sampling of those pieces run the gamut of topics. And, they do, indeed, reflect a microcosm of society:

1. In its June 9, 1980, issue, *The Chronicle* looked at the impact of the Supreme Court's ruling that faculty members at Yeshiva University were not entitled to bargain collectively. Yeshiva President Norman Lamm summed up the situation: "I had expected the sky to fall down. I thought if we won, we would have a massive disaffection with people crying in the classrooms. But life went on" (Watkins, 1980, p. 3).

2. Colleges also had to respond to federally issued mandates to accommodate handicapped students by modifying campus buildings and programs. *The Chronicle* found, in a review of many institutions, that colleges were reporting that the

necessary architectural changes could be made less expensively than they had expected (Hook, 1980, p. 15).

3. Social pressure as well as local ordinances brought problems surrounding smoking in the workplace to campuses in the mid-1980s. College personnel offices began drawing up policies to regulate smoking, *The Chronicle* reported. The significance of the issue, however, had not yet been recognized. The director of personnel at the University of Arizona, for example, said "It's very much a personnel policy, and not a health issue or anything else. Happy or not, we've reached an armed truce." That "truce" included an agreement whereby workers had swapped offices and cigar smokers had agreed to try cigarettes (Heller, 1984, p. 23).

There are hundreds of issues to be covered, according to *The Chronicle*'s editors. Some are inherited from the 1980s; some even go back to the 1970s; some spill over into questions of consumerism. Increasingly, colleges are going to have to spend more time explaining themselves.

Although *The Chronicle* is a voice of higher education, and its pages present many other voices of higher education, there has been a lack of dialogue from the leadership in the field, according to managing editor Scully (1992k). This seeming paradox results from what he calls a "crisis of belief in higher education."

"People are a little worried about making grand statements," he said. "I think that some people who are potential leaders are unwilling to come forward and take that profile."

Gwaltney added, "I think higher education does need voices, not a single voice. People suggest that *The Chronicle* step in and initiate an editorial page. That kind of comment does indicate a yearning for some kind of voice" (1992k). Yet more than two decades after he made the initial decision not to provide an editorial voice, Gwaltney continued to follow a strict adherence to the policy. And readers should not expect any list of "Best Colleges" or Top Educators" as might be found in the popular press.

"Even when my kids were ready to go to college, I was almost embarrassed," Gwaltney recalled (1992k). "I really did not feel qualified to judge what college my own children should be going to. I guided them by some extent by what we could afford. But we've got to avoid entanglements with institutions."

CHAPTER VII

READERS SPEAK OUT: SECTION 2 DEVELOPMENT

Opinion Pieces

Few magazines and newspapers in the country would refuse to sell their back pages, at premium rates, to advertisers. *The Chronicle*, however, reserved both section backs for editorial content. A *Point of View* piece has long anchored the back of Section 1, while *End Paper* was created to bring an artistic element to Section 2 shortly after the section became a separate pull-out in September 1987.

The Chronicle's editors regard the *Point of View* and *Opinion* pages as avenues to continue to cover stories that do not have a weekly breaking news angle. While most of the early pieces came in over the transom, pieces increasingly have been solicited on subjects of topical news interest and have truly stretched the thought-provoking nature of *The Chronicle*'s content. Over the years, authors have included numerous college and university presidents and chancellors, writers such as Ronnie Dugger, who penned *Our Invaded Universities* (1974, p. 16), government and association officials, and a wide variety of professors and scholars.

Since early in the publication's history, the format of *Point of View*, particularly, reflected publishing innovations—bound only, it seemed, by the print margins of the tabloid page. For example, *Point of View* took the form of poetry for William Ehrhart's "But the Pace Comes" in the November 29, 1971, issue (p. 8). The author, then a member of the class of 1973 at Swarthmore College, had composed the poem and printed it in a leaflet as a call to prospective students. The verse spoke of settling in:

> The pace comes;
> Not easily, not consciously (You can't turn your
> back on a book or it will bite you in the neck);
> It just seems to come
> Somewhere along in those first confused months.

Another *Point of View* (Williams, 1973, p. 16) was styled as a "Confidential Memorandum" to "Department Chairmen and Deans." The subject: "The Second Sex." In what appeared to be typewriter type, with unjustified margins, the author (who actually was director of the women's studies program and associate professor in the college of social and behavioral studies at the University of South Florida) laced the memorandum with humor and tongue-in-cheek references. For example, the memorandum suggested ways these administrators might avoid "flak" from their "women—your women faculty." The advice included suggestions that the administrators scrutinize their women faculty for any who might be a "ripe candidate" for promotion or a raise ("whichever will cost less") and who might have been overlooked for reasons such as: "Her husband has a good job so she doesn't need the money;" or "A comparable male needs the promotion more for career reasons." The memorandum ended with the observation that "it does happen once in a while that one of our gals does something noteworthy. . . . Do not neglect to recognize high achievement. At the very least, put a notice on the bulletin board. . . . Many women today are simply not satisfied with the old brotherly hug and pat on the fanny" (Williams, 1973, p. 16).

Sometimes, the editors of *The Chronicle* let photography speak its viewpoint. One such example is the May 8, 1972, issue, where *Point of View* captured scenes of anti-war demonstrations across the nation (Anti-war, p. 12). Christmas artwork usually dominates the page in the last issue of the calendar year. Artwork can also cover missteps, such as the nearly full-page drawing of a typical tourist pointing to a "Greetings from . . ." postcard on the *Point of View* page August 12, 1987. The caption explained the dilemma: "The author whose work was scheduled to appear in this space has sent us his manuscript: 'Having a wonderful vacation. Wish you were here.'"

The opinion pieces run the gamut of emotions and can, at the same time, be controversial and poignant. Again, *The Chronicle*'s editors experimented with format, such as the May 10, 1989, Section 2 opener (Howard, p. B1) composed with a photograph and a hand-written message. The contribution came from Billy Howard, a photographer at Emory University who, after his dentist died of AIDS in 1986 without ever telling his patients he was ill, assembled a book of portraits of people with AIDS. Each wrote a statement. The one appearing in *The Chronicle* read:

> The nights are the hardest. Sometimes I'm afraid to go to sleep—afraid that I may not wake up. Going to my support group has helped me. I can talk more openly about my illness now, but I still have fears. I'm afraid I may die all alone. What's more frightening is that no one will care.

Letters to the Editor

If Section 2 were a sentence, *Letters* would provide its punctuation. They are exclamatory, questioning, compound, and simple. A single article will elicit responses expressing dismay and delight.

Some letters contain stinging criticism. On *The Chronicle*'s portrayal of a college president's resignation as a "revolt," one writer opined: "The article . . . was regrettably inaccurate and a stain on the integrity and intelligence . . ." (Thrower, 1970, p. 4).

Others edit the publication. When *The Chronicle* reported that a university system's board of trustees had voted to "maintain a one-year surveillance of guest speakers invited to campuses," a department chairman mused if private investigators had been hired and suggested alternate language. *The Chronicle*'s editors responded: "We are maintaining a one-year surveillance on the guilty copyeditor" (Bornmann, 1971, p. 6).

As the publication matured, *The Chronicle* culled its influx of letters and requested they be kept within, first, a three hundred-word limit, and later, a five hundred-word limit. Space was not given to the less substantive, but laudatory remarks. Earlier letters, however, often expressed a reader's approval of *The Chronicle*. One faculty member responded to the coverage of her remarks to the National Collegiate Athletic Association convention with pleased surprise: "The accuracy of the report was impeccable. I am not accustomed to the superior reporting which you have afforded us" (Thorpe, 1972, p. 8).

Shakespeare, politics, pop-Marxism, accreditation, student aid, technology, tuition, admissions, firings, hirings, and, of course, death, taxes and a myriad of other topics have all been subjects of *The Chronicle*'s letter writing audience.

Although the axiom that truth is stranger than fiction usually holds true, *The Chronicle*, for a short time during the 1990 academic year, looked away from this premise to present an *Ask the Professor* column, alongside its readers' letters. The following example suffices to explain why the column was short-lived:

Dear Professor: As dean of arts and sciences at Iowa Occidental University, I have thirty-seven chairpersons clamoring for funds. How can I keep them all happy and still give out only 'merit' raises as my vice-president insists?
(Signed)
Harvey Birtvurst

Dear Mr. Birtvurst: You must be new at this. You couldn't keep them happy if the money supply were unlimited. Give each one the allotted pittance and tell them that it's more than so and so in drama or physics got, and that next year will be even better. Of course, they won't believe you, but they'll be so busy trying to work the same scam on faculty members in their own departments that they won't bother you again until next year.
(Signed)
"The Professor" (Ask, 1990, p. B4).

Over the years, several rules of thumb have been developed for the letters column:

1. Letters have to address something *The Chronicle* has published. Only letters addressing substantive content are used. Those which address English usage or other language technicality are passed on to Gwaltney, who often responds personally.

2. If someone criticizes an *Opinion* piece, the writer has a chance to rebut.

3. Letters are not published in response to other letters.

4. If there are several letters on one subject, they may be edited or cut for space reasons.

5. Reporters receive copies of letters. If the letter suggests an error in reporting, the situation is investigated before a decision is made to publish the letter.

End Paper **and More**

End Paper has evolved into an open window, almost without words, on the world of higher education. Even *The Chronicle*'s editors had difficulty defining the wide-ranging feature whose only requirement is a connection, often seemingly thin, with higher education.

Associate senior editor Gail Lewin characterized its origins as "typical Corbin" (Lewin, 1993). The editor wanted an arts component to Section 2, but no one, including Gwaltney, expressed a clear idea of its content or format. Lewin recalled a meeting of the publication's top editors at which she presented a myriad of ideas. She was greeted with silence. Nobody knew what anybody else wanted. And deadline was drawing closer. Finally, they decided to combine a piece on William Wordsworth, excerpted from an upcoming book of essays with a notice of a new traveling exhibition entitled "William Wordsworth and the Age of English Romanticism." One week down. What were they going to do the next week?

What they did was dig in the proverbial trash. Gwaltney previously had rejected the use of a touching, rather poetic letter written by artist Georgia O'Keeffe to Derek Bok, then president of Harvard University, after O'Keeffe had received an honorary doctorate degree in 1973. The editor's rejection did not reflect on the letter's quality; there was simply not a format for such an item. Or was there?

The letter to Bok, two photographs of O'Keeffe and a notice of a traveling exhibition featuring her works composed the second *End Paper* in the November 4, 1987, issue (*End*, 1987a, p. B60). Then came a poem by Richard Wilbur, "For the Student Strikers," (*End*, 1987b, p. B60), along with the notation that the poet was the recently designated Poet Laureate of the United States. Any preconception of the feature had given way to imagination. Structure had given way to substance.

Visual impact became the hallmark of *End Paper*, achieved through illustration, photography, white space, or unusual type treatments. Topics have included culture, politics, and fashion. News is sought about exhibitions in cities where academic conventions are being held, and the page remains doggedly uncommercial. No catalog prices are included nor purchase information regarding books. Still, the creatively intriguing feature remains difficult to define, even for Gwaltney. When asked, he paused, and with typical understatement, offered, "Eclectic is a word that comes to mind" (Gwaltney, 1993b).

Gwaltney has viewed the evolution of Section 2 and its opinion pieces, letters, and other features as a way to get readers, especially faculty, involved in the publication. More mail is received on *Opinion*, he said, than any other feature. "It's wonderful to stir up readers," Gwaltney said (1993b). "These are people who pick up their pens or word processors and let us know what they think."

Readers unexpectedly responded when, starting with the June 30, 1993, issue, Section 2, which is folded into the newspaper at the center spread of Section 1, began appearing upside down. The printing tactic was intended to make Section 2 easier to find and pull out.

Over the years, Gwaltney had tried various methods to distinguish Section 2 from the first section, including directional arrows, to instruct the reader to separate the sections. The calls and letters began immediately. Readers thought some mistake had been made. They thought they had been singled out. One asked if Section 2 were right side up and the first section upside down. They seemed to find the action disorienting, reported associate publisher William D. Criger (1993).

Finally, after nearly three months, with the calls and letters continuing, Gwaltney focused on the subject in the *Marginalia* column, his weekly humorous look at higher education's people, places, events, communications, and "bloopers." He reported that one reader from New York City wrote: "I would like to know what's happening. Is someone asleep at the wheel? Is technology imposing a new and bizarre requirement? Are you testing the alertness of readers? Or is the upsidedownness meant to convey some sort of message? Please let me know the score. Meanwhile, I find it extremely difficult to read Section 2 in its present position." Another complained that the action was driving him "bonkers." Gwaltney explained his reasoning in *Marginalia*, and apologized the explanation was so "simple—and that dull" (Gwaltney, 1993p, p. A6).

Sometimes, however, *The Chronicle*'s responsiveness just is not adequate satisfaction for readers. One of Gwaltney's favorite stories is about the reader who called with a complaint and, still dissatisfied with the editor's response, asked to speak to his boss.

"I am the boss," Gwaltney replied.

"I mean your boss," the reader countered.

"I am my boss," Gwaltney tried again.

The caller hung up (Gwaltney, 1993l).

CHAPTER VIII

BEHIND THE HEADLINES: THE EVOLUTION OF UNITED STATES HIGHER EDUCATION

Collegiate Trends, Friends, and Critics

Other than his initials on the *Marginalia* column, editor Corbin Gwaltney has had one byline in *The Chronicle*. The byline came early in the publication's history and it reflected the stature of the story's subject: Clark Kerr, at the time newly ousted as University of California president. The article with Gwaltney's byline was such a singular event that, years later, he had to refer to past issues to remember the incident. The story with his name carried a dateline of New York and was the news coverage of Kerr's appointment by the Carnegie Foundation for the Advancement of Teaching to the chairmanship of a commission formed to conduct a three- to six-year study of the future structure and financing of all phases of United States higher education (Gwaltney, 1967, p. 1).

"I had a particularly good pipeline into the people mentioned— probably better than anybody in the country so I guess that's why I did it," Gwaltney said (1993h), adding, "We did not have a big staff in those days."

But a note from Gwaltney to Kerr gave further insight. The letter, which briefly lifted the veil from Gwaltney's seemingly unwavering journalistic objectivity, is as singular in the editor's file as the byline in his newspaper. Although undated, the letter was likely written in early 1980 when the Kerr-led Carnegie Council on Policy Studies in Higher Education (the successor to the Carnegie Commission) issued its final report, which included a look ahead to the year 2000 and the expected problems and issues for higher education (Scully, 1980, p. 1). Further corroboration of this dating supposition comes from the letterhead's New Hampshire Avenue address, home to *The Chronicle* from 1979 through 1984. The letter read:

> Dear Clark:
>
> Everyone's yardstick will be different, as we try to measure—and then tell you—how much you have meant to us. Mine, inevitably, has a lot to do with your presence in the columns of this newspaper, over the years.
>
> No one else comes close to the number of column inches that you and your work have occupied in *The Chronicle of Higher Education*. Week after week, your work in Berkeley has been the higher education story, as our front pages attest.
>
> Indeed, you were in the very first Page One "lead" story that *The Chronicle of Higher Education* ever published. There have been some weeks in which, without the articles about you and your colleagues at the Carnegie Commission and the Carnegie Council, we would have been hard put to find just the right 'important' story with which to lead our paper.
>
> Thus, for us in this office, your position as the leading figure in higher education is an unquestionable fact. Subjectively, of course, we knew it all along!
>
> > All best,
> > (Signed "Corbin")
> > Corbin Gwaltney

Harvard University Press obviously concurs with Gwaltney's assessment of Kerr's leadership within the higher education community. For both the ensuing decades of the 1970s and the 1980s, since the publication of Kerr's *The Uses of the University* in 1963, the publisher requested the president emeritus of the University of California to prepare a revised epilogue for a new edition of the book. For its latest edition, the Press wanted an updated preface discussing the 1990s and beyond.

This pending writing task was on the octogenarian's mind as he sat in his unairconditioned office at the Institute of Industrial Relations, just south of the Berkeley campus, late on a June afternoon in 1993. He reflected on higher education's past, during the quarter century-plus of *The Chronicle*'s publishing history, and pondered what he might write about the next twenty years in higher education's evolution. No doubt, the issues Kerr writes about also will find their ways into the pages of *The Chronicle*. And an understanding of such issues puts *The Chronicle*'s history into perspective.

Kerr recalled that, in 1968, in *Agenda for the Nation*, he wrote that "higher education in the United States is at the pinnacle of its effectiveness. It is also more beset with more fundamental problems than ever before in its history" (Kerr, 1968, p. 237).

"That's still the situation," he said (Kerr, 1993). "Higher education in the United States is still at the pinnacle of its effectiveness despite problems. Compared with its own history and compared with countries all over the world, United States higher education provides more access to young people. We also give them more choice. We have a tremendous variety of public as well as private institutions. And our research, from a quantitative point of view, is probably the greatest in the world."

Kerr suggested that few would disagree that graduate training in the United States also is the best and creates one of the country's few trade surpluses. The nation receives some $5 billion a year from graduate students from around the world, he said, more than the country spends on United States students studying abroad (Kerr, 1993).

"We also have a remarkable record in supplying the labor market. In most countries, higher education lags behind. It doesn't produce enough engineers until it becomes fully evident that they are needed. Our education has been ahead of the demand. We've anticipated the need for engineers and business managers. So our labor market has been clearly the most responsive among the major industrial countries in the world and probably all countries," he said (Kerr, 1993).

Still, the educator stressed, higher education has experienced cycles of fundamental problems, and basic secular trends have impacted its evolution. The 1960s witnessed an increase in the federal government's involvement in new programs, student aid, and research. The 1960s, of course, also brought dramatic confrontation to the nation's campuses. Colleges and universities became battlegrounds around the morality of national intervention in Vietnam. In addition, the civil rights movement and growing dissatisfaction by women with their traditional roles made the period one of mere survival.

The 1970s experienced a loss of energy and decline in spirit as well as diminished vision. For the first time since World War II, with the 1974 depression, colleges and universities were confronting retrenchment and fiscal realignment. The depression also seemed to bring a sense of disillusionment internally about the prospects for higher education and externally as to the degree that institutions could be trusted to deliver on the euphoric hopes of the post-World War II period.

The 1980s, according to Kerr, brought a relatively non-historical period of status quo continuum. A predicted demographic depression did not materialize because a higher proportion of young people decided to go to college. The Cold War, which focused on scientific research for military purposes, shifted to what Kerr called the Cold Peace, with emphasis on research for the sake of economic competition. The Cold Peace also has brought a shift in focus from basic research and research universities to polytechnic research or more applied research.

Institutions sought to renew their vitality, but as the decade of the 1980s waned they became faced with ideological battles, fueled by external critics who began to wonder whether universities were anything other than self-serving introspective places. Among the harsh critiques was Allan Bloom's *The Closing of the American Mind,* which concluded that going to college does not mean an education will be achieved (1987).

The same year, Ernest Boyer published *College: The Undergraduate Experience in America* (1987), which showed that full-time students represented a shrinking portion of the college population. In fact, according to this report, the number of part-time students had grown to constitute nearly one-third of enrollments in four-year colleges.

Boyer, president of the Carnegie Foundation for the Advancement of Teaching, in Princeton, New Jersey, said he believes that colleges and universities stand on the threshold of trying to redefine their answer to the critics. He also views the renewal attempt as their response to a new century.

"The lines of that renewal are not yet clearly established," he said (Boyer, 1993). "I've sensed several themes that have emerged in the redefinition of higher education. Certainly, there is a rediscovery of the importance of the undergraduate, which I think is long overdue and has been neglected since World War II."

A parallel to the undergraduate education debate, he added, is a reexamination of the faculty reward system, with many espousing that faculty should be rewarded, not just for the scholarship of discovery, but for the scholarship of integrating, applying, and transmitting knowledge.

"At the same time, an important point should be made," Boyer said (1993). "I think there's been a growing feeling that higher education is more for the private benefit than for the public good. And that's a major shift from World War II when we really did think of higher education as being in the nation's service. Now we see it as a place where faculty get tenured and students get credentialed. But that doesn't have much to do with helping to resolve the nation's pressing problems."

That private benefit–public good debate will influence who pays for higher education in the future, Boyer said. If it is a private benefit, then students should pay, goes the reasoning. That sentiment, Boyer noted, has led, in recent years, to the most dramatic expansion in tuition in the last fifty years.

Boyer summed up the current status of higher education as "sobering reassessment. I think it is a rediscovery of undergraduate education. It is a rethinking of the role of the professoriate, and, I might add, it is a reawakening of the question of what is the university's role in terms of service" (Boyer, 1993).

Future Challenges

A couple of years ago, Kerr was at Columbia University in New York to visit a longtime friend when the friend asked if there was someone else Kerr wanted to see. Kerr answered with a professor's name. His friend said, "You know, I think I've heard of him, but I don't know the individual. Let's go the office, and the secretary will look him up" (Kerr, 1993).

The secretary informed the two that said professor occupied the office next to Kerr's acquaintance. The incident affirmed Kerr's concept of the "multiversity," the idea that a large university is "a whole series of communities and activities held together by a common name, a common governing board, and related purposes" (Kerr, 1968, p. 1). The educator first introduced the term in the early 1960s.

"I think there has been a continuing disintegration of the sense of community in the university," he said. "There are faculty members who are a lot closer, via the fax machine, with colleagues elsewhere than they are to the guy in the office next door" (Kerr, 1993). Today, Kerr said, members of a university community are more likely to be tied together by a budget and common grievances over parking.

They are also linked by *The Chronicle.* An early study of the newspaper's rapid initial success concluded that the publication's growth, via paid subscriptions, reflected the extent that it provided information useful in decision making and other administrative functions (Currie, 1975, p. 321). The continuing fractionalization that Kerr foresees can only mean increasing information needs for those in academe, from students to administrators.

"The humanities are just torn apart," Kerr said (1993), by the divisions among gender, race, ethnic group, and ideology. "The fractionalization is probably the greatest that has come about since 'science versus religion' during and after the Civil War," he suggested (Kerr, 1993).

Kerr identified, however, the greatest future challenge as the shortage of resources to support higher education. "We're struggling to get resources as we never had to in previous times. Almost all states are cutting back," he said (1993). "The battle for resources, I think, is going to actually intensify, although people on the firing line say it's the worst ever."

Contributing to the tightening of resources, Kerr said, is the federal government's shift from student support based upon need to student support based upon politics. He said that by essentially adding the middle income student to the assistance pool, the government has significantly increased costs as well as created an increasing emphasis from grants to loans.

"If I were going to pick what history will say about 1990 to 2010, it would be the period of the biggest struggle to get resources that public higher education has ever had in American history," Kerr said (1993). He added that, in a nation with a quarter of all children born and raised in poverty, higher education has difficulty in staking a greater claim on resources than the health of the population or the welfare of children.

"There are new competitors [for resources] coming along," he said (1993). The result for higher education will be a pitting of department against department; school against school; administration, trustees and the individual institution against the governor and the legislature. He concluded the future will be a "wrenching" period. Or, as a chancellor in Oklahoma once told him, "The corrals are getting smaller, the barbed wire is getting higher" (Kerr, 1993).

Political Environment

The fall of 1986 brought quintessential meetings of higher education and politics. September marked Harvard University's 350th birthday as the nation's oldest higher education institution. The university tried to plan, *The Chronicle* reported, a modest "family" celebration. So much for planning. Prince Charles of Great Britain attended, but President Ronald Reagan, "presumably miffed because a number of faculty members opposed his receiving an honorary degree," did not (Ingalls, 1986, p. 1).

The family feuding did not stop with the celebration. Within weeks, Harvard alumnus and Education Secretary William J. Bennett charged, in a speech delivered at Harvard, that college and university officials were more concerned with money than education and had not done enough to make sure students learn anything before they graduate. *The Chronicle* called Bennett's speech the "most comprehensive statement of his views on higher education since he took office" (Palmer, 1986, p. 1). Derek C. Bok, president of Harvard, called Bennett's speech "superficial" and said it failed to consider many facts about United States higher education. Typical of *The Chronicle*'s news presentation style, full texts of both Bennett's and Bok's remarks accompanied the article.

The same week as the Bennett and Bok exchange, Robert H. Atwell, president of the American Council on Education, accused the Reagan Administration of encouraging an "unregulated pursuit of self-interest" in the country and of making a "diminished commitment to investing in the overall good" (Education, 1986, p. 1). *The Chronicle* quoted Atwell: "By defining the common good as national defense, this Administration has rationalized abandoning those unable to compete and has chosen guns over butter" (Education, 1986, p. 1).

Of course, the churning of politics and higher education under a Reagan Administration was nothing new. Not only was he the California governor who fired Clark Kerr, but he also campaigned for the presidency in 1980 with a campaign pledge to abolish the Department of Education. Terrel Bell, appointed Secretary of Education, was to make sure it happened.

The department was not abolished, and Bell, an education consultant and professor at the University of Utah, later wrote *The Thirteenth Man* (1988) about his frustrating four years in the Cabinet. The title connotes the order of Bell's last-to-be-appointed post as well as his odd-man-out status among peers who considered him a short-timer. Bell brought unusual experience and perspective about higher education and government to the position. He most immediately prior to Reagan's appointment had been commissioner of the Utah system of higher education. He also represented the "E" in the former Department of Health, Education and Welfare during several years of the Nixon and Ford Administrations in the 1970s.

Bell finished his latest government experience with more defined opinions about the media, including *The Chronicle*, where his photograph and activities appeared frequently, starting with his confirmation hearing in January 1981. The article, which also included a mention of the last major appearance of outgoing Education Secretary Shirley M. Hufstedler, concluded that the rhetoric from the two appearances "demonstrated the distance between the philosophical and political perspectives of the Carter and Reagan Administrations on education issues" (Fields and Hook, 1981, p. 1).

"I felt *The Chronicle* was quite fair," Bell said, although "not at the outset—I think it was the situation." Bell said he had to "earn" his way with *The Chronicle*, which he characterized (although noting he did not like labels) as "liberal," an attitude that "makes it tough when you have to advocate the boss' position [in a Republican Administration]" (Bell, 1993).

Bell said that *The Chronicle* was circulated during his tenure at the Department of Education at least through the level of director, those managers below the assistant secretary level who have responsibility for a specific program. In many regards, he said, *The Chronicle* was more helpful to him in his federal post than as a state education commissioner. He commended the publication for its coverage of national issues, such as student financial aid, and its presentation of both positive and negative commentary.

Still, when it came to dealing with Congress, Bell said, he paid more attention to the mass media, especially the *New York Times*, the *Washington Post*, and the *Wall Street Journal*. "In Washington, the media affects perceptions, and in Washington, perception is almost everything," he said. "An article in the *Wall Street Journal* highlighting certain problems in higher education would cause you to brace to respond and defend" (Bell, 1993).

Scott Jaschik, associate managing editor for national news at *The Chronicle*, said that the priorities of the administration in power in Washington will affect what *The Chronicle* covers because those issues will garner the most time and attention from government officials. For example, the Clinton Administration's national service proposal has been a focus of *The Chronicle*'s reporting efforts.

Jaschik said there are also issues that *The Chronicle* will cover whether an administration designates them as priorities or not. With President Bill Clinton, *The Chronicle* has in the White House a man who has been interviewed by at least three of its reporters. One article by Jaschik in 1986 (p. 25) quoted the then-Arkansas Governor in support of higher education: "To have real economic growth, we're going to have to produce more, better-educated people."

But as one Washington insider noted, the nation's capital city is "90 percent exchanging gossip and information. And the memory fades." Gwaltney has long been aware of the dangers of Washington politics and the tendency of journalists to be swept in by the activities "inside the Beltway."

In 1969, as the newspaper was about to become a weekly, he wrote a confidential analysis criticizing his own product as appearing to have a "pet interest" in the affairs of Washington-based education associations as well as perhaps too heavily dipping into its ink to cover every bill introduced in Congress that might influence or affect colleges and universities. The internal assessment made it clear that Gwaltney planned to place new emphasis on news in higher education, not just around it.

Chapter IX

The Campus Beat: The Journalistic Environment

Competitive Trends

"You just don't understand," the television reporter argued with Clark Kerr, then president of the University of California. "None of us think we're reporting history. We're in entertainment" (Kerr, 1993).

The exchange came in a Burbank, California, television studio during the mid-1960s as the growing freedom of speech movement gained momentum on the Berkeley campus. Kerr had complained to the reporter that television was reporting "exaggerations" (Kerr, 1993).

"When we had troubles at Berkeley," he later recalled, "you would think nothing else was happening on the campus. The students were spectacular in the way they handled TV."

Kerr claimed that only five percent of the students were involved in the protests, at least initially, and he unsuccessfully attempted to shift some focus to the remaining ninety-five percent. The educator was not alone in his criticisms of the mass media in the 1960s. In his report to the Carnegie Corporation of New York, Editorial Projects for Education Chairman Wolk (1963) put No. 1 on his list of "Highlights" the fact that "From education's own leadership—professionals as well as laymen—to the general public, Americans are not well-informed about higher education" (p. 1). Wolk went on to conclude that this fact appeared to be at least partially responsible for many of higher education's problems, including its difficulties with legislation and in obtaining public support. He claimed that the general public received "relatively little solid information about higher education" (p. 1) from newspapers, popular magazines, and television. He further stated that few newspaper writers or editors had higher education as their major assignment and that the problem was being perpetuated because "few well-trained people are entering the field of education reporting. Almost nothing is being done to increase the supply" (p 1).

By late 1993, the Washington, D.C.-based Education Writers Association had 317 active members in forty states, the District of Columbia, and Canada. Lisa J. Walker, executive director, said it is difficult to determine by titles how many members actually write about higher education as part of their jobs. She reported, however, that the association is planning to conduct research to obtain better information and statistics on its membership (Walker, 1993). Still, the journalistic situation is such that *Educational Record* magazine warned its readers, members of the American Council on Education, that "most news organizations today are ill-prepared to write about higher education. . . . Work to educate the media" (Bowler, 1988, p. 9).

The competitive environment created by the mass media, or, more aptly, the lack of competitive environment, left the proverbial gate wide open for *The Chronicle*, according to Reese Cleghorn, dean of the University of Maryland's College of Journalism and president of the *American Journalism Review*. Still, he added, higher education remains a "terribly neglected beat with very few people who know how to cover it." *The Chronicle* has not taken the competitive environment for granted. By 1993, the newspaper had thirty-six people in its 161-person staff box with the word "editor" in their titles. Every facet of higher education had become a beat of its own at the specialized newspaper.

Cleghorn (1993) offered the experience of a longtime journalist and an academic of more than twelve years: "It's just obvious to me that nobody bothers to learn how higher education works before covering it. When a story comes up, all they know how to do is call the president. Or, if it's athletics, they'll call the athletic director, then the president."

He suggested that higher education reporters need the same beat familiarity as a city hall reporter, who spends substantial time with sources and who knows the ones who will "talk straight" and the ones who will not. Cleghorn recalled the culture of the newsroom during his reporting days:

> I wanted to be a political reporter. I wanted to cover city hall, the court house, the state capitol. That's how I became assistant city editor. That's the way you did it. Women often got put on the education beat for reasons of second class citizenship. There also was some surmise that they might know more about schools. That was the orphan beat. The orphan of the orphan, higher education, was even lower than that (Cleghorn, 1993).

Higher education remains, for the most, a secondary part of the school reporter's beat, and even that beat does not often include the politics of education. When the state board of regents or the state board of education takes an action, the story often is covered by a political reporter rather than an expert in education (Cleghorn, 1993).

Cleghorn has been amazed that *The Chronicle* has not drawn direct competition. "I'm not sure what it is parallel to in other industries. It kind of occupies the territory, and there's not any real alternative," he said. "In our field (communications), nobody fully occupies all the territory. If you want a classified ad, you go to *Editor & Publisher*. If you want another kind of time with the reader, you go to us (*American Journalism Review*) or *Columbia Journalism Review*. If you want something else, you might go to *Adweek*" (Cleghorn, 1993).

Harvard University social scientist David Riesman, prolific author on higher education and a former member of the Carnegie Commission on Higher Education, views *The Chronicle* in a sociological context. One of the things *The Chronicle* has done, according to Riesman (1993), is to nationalize higher education.

"It has widened the orbit," Riesman (1993) said, noting that the expanded view of the higher education community comes not just from the editorial content but also from the national scope, indeed international scope, of the classified job listings.

He pointed to research in the 1960s that showed most college and university presidents were located where they grew up, where they had studied, or where they were when they received their presidential appointment. That, he said, is no longer the case. *The Chronicle's* influence has been part of what Riesman calls the "diversity industry." Its news pages and position openings say to an institution, "You have to get somebody different, or at least consider somebody different" (Riesman, 1993).

Riesman, who gained early prominence with his 1950 book, *The Lonely Crowd: A Study of the Changing American Character*, has written extensively on college presidents. He once told a *Washington Post* reporter that the "changing constellation" of university leaders to ones more preoccupied with the financial vulnerability of the institutions has left a void in American society. Riesman told the *Post* writer: "What we lose as a country are people with visible credibility and intelligence and integrity who can tell us things we don't want to hear, but need to hear" (Jordan, 1992, p. 1A).

"It's an odd thing," Riesman said. "With all its talk about diversity, *The Chronicle* is actually making higher education, as an arena, more homogeneous" (1993).

Daily Reporting

As he sat in his office at the University of Maryland at College Park, surrounded by clippings from *The Chronicle of Higher Education*, Howard Bray remembered his first and only three-martini lunch. As director of the Knight Center for Specialized Journalism, he was in the midst of planning for an October 1993 conference on higher education writing. Outlining the program brought back memories of that lunch a couple of decades earlier when he was a young journalist in Louisville, Kentucky. His city editor used the lunch to convince him to cover education.

The fall 1993 conference represented the University of Maryland's second effort to advance the field of higher education reporting. The first was in the fall of 1983, when Maryland's College of Journalism conducted a study supported by a grant from the Exxon Education Foundation. The major conclusions of the study were published in *Journalism Educator* in the Winter of 1985 (Yarrington, p. 11). These included:

1. Most writers covering higher education also cover elementary and secondary education; very few cover higher education exclusively.

2. Many education writers have other responsibilities, such as covering news about women, automobiles, real estate, entertainment, and gardening.

3. Of the 1,730 U.S. daily newspapers, fewer than 250 list an education writer or editor. Papers with circulations under ten thousand show more education writers than papers with circulations over twenty thousand.

4. Most writers assigned to education do not stay long. Neither they nor their editors consider it a long-time assignment or a career specialty.

5. Reporters with national reputations as higher education writers tend to come from papers that have a commitment to the coverage of post-secondary education.

6. The top higher education writers have a high personal interest in reporting education. Several consider it a professional specialty to which they are committed and would not change to other assignments if asked.

7. Leading practitioners tend to write about two to three higher education stories a week. Most common topics are finance, organization, and curriculum (Yarrington, 1985, p. 11).

Bray's anecdotal research, he said, tells him that newsrooms have not changed much in the ensuing decade. "Because newsrooms are essentially divided up into different territories, sometimes pieces fall through the cracks, and there may not be a great deal of coherence," Bray said (1993).

Fred Hechinger, a senior adviser for the Carnegie Corporation of New York and former education editor for the *New York Times*, agreed, "As long as news managers don't put much emphasis on education, reporters will try to get out [of the beat]" (1993).

Hechinger started covering education stories in Europe after World War II for a now defunct news agency. The visibility resulted in the *New York Herald Tribune*'s education editor asking him to do a series of reviews of the educational systems of different countries. When the editor left the *Tribune*, Hechinger got the job. In 1956, he left the *Tribune* to manage a newspaper in Connecticut for three years. In 1959, he joined the *Times* and became education editor a decade later, a post he held for nearly another decade. At one point in his tenure, he had a staff of five reporters.

"I have to say, the *Times* doesn't have five now," he said (Hechinger, 1993). "When I was education editor, I fought very hard every day to keep the department together and to get space. I felt very strongly about it, and I didn't hesitate to fight. My theory about it is unless you make a very special effort to persuade them, the news managers don't have much interest in education" (1993).

Hechinger noted, too, that his staff was not larger because of the era of campus riots, usually covered by other reporters. "I used to say that when I went to Columbia (University) during an uprising," Hechinger remembered, "the first ten people I'd meet were not college rebels, but *Times* reporters" (Hechinger, 1993).

Peer Review

A visit to the library of the American Council on Education in One Dupont Center in Washington, D.C.—where education publications line the shelved walls—provides evidence that *The Chronicle* is a unique journalistic undertaking. The newspaper is also one of the most cited higher education publications.

For example, in a study of 569 articles published during a six-year period in the three core journals of higher education—*Journal of Higher Education, Research in Higher Education,* and *Review of Higher Education—The Chronicle* was the eleventh most frequently cited publication, with 123 citations (Budd, 1990, p. 91). Heading the list was *Research in Higher Education,* with 492 citations. When subsequently contacted, the author of the article said that a proprietary data base management program was developed for the study, making it difficult to duplicate, but that there were "no real surprises" and that other researchers had "confirmed the prejudices" reflected in the article (Budd, 1992).

In this country, *The Chronicle*'s closest competitors during its first quarter-century have been *Change, Educational Record, Black Issues in Higher Education,* and *Lingua franca.* Each, however, was established with a very different editorial presentation or offered a very different journalistic focus from *The Chronicle*'s, as the following brief descriptions indicate.

1. *Change.* Owned and published bi-monthly by Heldref Publications, under the editorial direction of the American Association for Higher Education, *Change* is subtitled *The Magazine of Higher Learning.* Launched in January, 1969, by the New York-based consulting firm of Science and University Affairs, *Change* was financed by a $275,000 grant from the Esso Education Foundation (Magazine, 1968). The glossy magazine emphasizes issues and was founded to, and continues to, reflect the changes occurring in higher education.

2. *Educational Record.* This quarterly magazine of the American Council on Education is, by its own description, "concerned with the broad range of issues affecting higher education." As part of an advocacy group in higher education, however, the magazine does not provide an independent voice of journalism.

3. *Black Issues in Higher Education.* Published in Fairfax, Virginia, this national, biweekly publication is devoted to

covering minority participation in higher education. The magazine-sized, newsprint publication is accompanied, six times a year, by a special report on issues in higher education. Because of its minority focus, the publication receives substantial business in its classified advertising of job openings.

4. *Lingua franca.* This bimonthly magazine describes itself as the "review of academic life" and says it offers "no-holds-barred shoptalk." Generally targeted toward faculty in the humanities, *Lingua franca* completed its third year of publication with its September/October 1993 issue. In the spring of 1993, the publication won a prestigious National Magazine Award for general excellence in the circulation category of "under 100,000." In a news release announcing the award sponsored by the American Society of Magazine Editors and administered by the Graduate School of Journalism at Columbia University, the judges said the magazine "ventures well beyond the ivory tower and writes in a tone that is irreverent, if not downright sassy, and showcases the imaginative articles in a classic and elegant design."

Russell Edgerton, president of the American Association for Higher Education and chairman of the Editorial Group for *Change* magazine, called *The Chronicle* a "major institution" of higher education. At the same time, however, he said its size—"too big and flabby" —hinders the newspaper from having a clear focus. He would prefer to see less on politics, more on quality issues in higher education (Edgerton, 1993).

Of course, everyone has an editorial preference. Educator Clark Kerr would like to see more "in-depth" articles and more book reviews (1993). Foundation chief Ernest Boyer would like *The Chronicle* to take editorial stands. *Change* magazine executive editor Theodore Marchese, would like more coverage of academic affairs. But as one *Chronicle* staff member noted, with the assurance of anonymity, a newspaper is not a democracy.

CHAPTER X

THE BLUE WALL: DESIGN AND PRODUCTION

Thursdays at the "Wall"

A large clock sits high on the blue-gray wall that runs some twenty-five feet along one side of *The Chronicle*'s production area. Other than the clock, printed numbers and hooks, destined to hold dummied layout pages, are all that claim the wall, until Thursday. Thursday is deadline day at *The Chronicle*. With two sections, an increasing number of pages, and imposing color requirements, deadline is an all-day and a long-day affair.

A noon deadline is targeted for Section 2 pages, with a 7 P.M. deadline giving the first section's breaking news the greatest leeway for last-minute changes. A miniature page dummy is pinned to a bulletin board on a far wall of the production area, showing that "This Week's Issue" has 128 pages, about average for *The Chronicle*'s latest editions. By mid-morning, columns of set type hang from the hooks, awaiting paste-up by three production artists. A few completed dummies await approval. Each layout dummy page is printed with a series of check-off boxes showing that the page has had a final proof reading, its jump checked, its headline approved, its page numbers verified, section head approval, Malcolm Scully's initialed okay, and last, but not least, the blessing of the initials "C. G."

The Chronicle's editor is omnipresent on deadline day. And the few he misses seem only to add to the pressure to strive for perfection. "He (Gwaltney) is unique in his presence—and absence," one staff member observed. No hour is too late for a hyphen to be added or a headline word modified. He reads every word in every issue. He is quick to praise; quick to criticize; quick to re-think any part of any page. These attributes of a perfectionist led *Change* magazine to characterize Gwaltney as "the chief persnickety" in a 1983 report on the newspaper (Connell and Yarrington, p. 20).

With ten pages of crime statistics and a staff writer covering a National Collegiate Athletic Association (NCAA) convention an hour behind Washington time in Dallas, this particular deadline day portends a late closing. Scully carries a clip board as a constant reminder of deadline status. He shepherds the final countdown.

5:30 P.M. The quotations in the *Quote, Unquote* column on the cover are checked against page numbers. The contents items are checked.

5:43 P.M. Staff members are milling in the production area, making movement somewhat difficult. Scully talks to the reporter in Dallas, editing the story on the computer terminal in front of him via long distance. Before he hangs up, he tells the reporter to call again in forty-five minutes, in case there are additional questions.

5:52 P.M. Edith Taylor, librarian, *Gazette* editor, and grammar specialist on deadline day, makes a final ruling on a grammatical question.

5:56 P.M. The final boards of the statistical listing are ready, then not ready. Editors find mistakes.

6:05 P.M. Someone questions the spelling of the name "Nelsen." Is it Nelson? The reporter is called for verification.

6:08 P.M. The reporter in Dallas calls. Scully reads him the headline on the NCAA story. They confer on a change.

6:17 P.M. An initial capital letter, a cut-in letter, is discovered missing. The story must be cut to accommodate what has become a larger lead, or opening paragraph.

6:26 P.M. A production artist is still repairing typographical errors with "patches."

6:30 P.M. The reporter in Dallas calls again with an addition to his story.

6:33 P.M. Deadline is late, with twenty-two pages left, including the ten sheets of crime statistics.

6:34 P.M. Quickly, staff members start to move the statistical pages off their hooks as they receive final approval.

6:36 P.M. Another headline word is changed.

6:38 P.M. The production area is full and humming with nearly twenty voices.

6:44 P.M. Eleven pages left.

6:55 P.M. The final corrections for the NCAA article are pasted on waiting boards.

7:08 P.M. Seven pages left.

7:14 P.M. Four pages left.

7:19 P.M. Final initials to the last pages. Scully checks who is assigned to go to the printer the following day.

7:22 P.M. The blue-gray wall once again becomes empty. The production area becomes quiet. Only the clock remains, marking the countdown until the next Thursday.

From Front Page to Cover

To newspaper traditionalists in the 1960s, "beauty" of design was gray simplicity à la the *New York Times*. Column upon column of type was broken up only by the occasional photograph and staid headline. *The Chronicle*'s first look mimicked the nation's newspaper of record, although in *The Chronicle*'s case, the one-column photographs and the greater number of words than illustrations came largely as a product of sheer economics. The photographs in the earliest issues were usually handouts from college public relations offices. And, with only eight pages, space for larger photographs was a luxury the newspaper could ill afford.

Still, there was a self-sense of beauty. An admitted "type-ophile," Gwaltney insisted the newspaper use a typeface for its headlines called Bulmer, a font he had earlier made the official typeface of the Johns Hopkins publications. Bulmer was not used in general circulation newspapers because of the many cursive elements that not only made its look distinctive, but also broke off in the days of hot metal type. To get Bulmer later in phototype, *The Chronicle*'s editors had to issue an ultimatum to the manufacturers of the typesetting machines: "Provide Bulmer or we won't buy your typesetters" (Gwaltney, 1993n).

Volume II made its debut with two-column cartoons on the front page, again a function of balancing economic resources with the desire for a larger art element. By 1969, the photographs were getting larger and often used in series of three, making the photography element more dominant on the page. The year 1971 brought a design experiment in placing a story, bordered with a rounded box, above the masthead—a style short-lived because the mailing label often blocked the ability to read the lead story.

Because of printing requirements, *The Chronicle* has been published in three sizes. The earliest dimensions were 13 inches by 17 3/4 inches. In 1973, the newspaper shrunk to a page size of 11 inches by 16 7/8 inches. In 1978, the newspaper switched to what has become a standard tabloid size in printing, 11 inches by 14 3/4 inches.

Summer editions, particularly, lent themselves to what Gwaltney called "tinkering." The summer of 1976 brought full-page drawings to the front page, commemorating "Great Moments in Higher Education" and offering what the subtitle explained as "*The Chronicle*'s own Bicentennial history." The originals of this pen-and-ink artwork still hang in *The Chronicle*'s office lobby. Gwaltney said he is most proud of having the idea of Thomas Jefferson's measuring the bald head of Benjamin Franklin in order to get a design for the rotunda at the University of Virginia (June 28, 1976).

Another drawing, however, brought the Johns Hopkins alumnus the wrath of his alma mater. The illustration (July 26, 1976) showed professors coming off a boat, depicting the fact that Johns Hopkins is credited with importing the concept of the German university. In the drawing, the ship bore the name *horst vessel*, a christening that angered Johns Hopkins President Steven Muller, whose complaint call saying that the similarly pronounced *Horstwessel* referred to a Nazi war criminal, came shortly after the newspaper arrived in subscriber mailboxes. The faux pas brought an unusual print apology from Gwaltney (1993n).

The summer issues of 1977 used three-column, full-length portraits on the cover, a harbinger of *The Chronicle*'s cover look of the early 1990s. Beginning in the fall of 1977, the front pages often carried a single story, sometimes two or three, with headlines getting larger and white space being used more generously. The *News Summary* and contents listing, however, which had been added in 1974, continued in the far left column and helped the page retain its news-orientation. The layout design stayed relatively consistent into the 1980s, with the later 1980s seeing a return to an increased number of articles on the front page. In September 1991, *The Chronicle* traded its front-page *News Summary* for page three's *This Week in The Chronicle*, a comprehensive listing and summary of the issue's contents. In place of the *News Summary* on the front page came *Quote, Unquote*, a selection of provocative quotes from within the issue's stories. In the Summer of 1992, *The Chronicle* eased to a greater degree into a magazine look with a three-column photograph anchoring what the editors started calling the "cover." Gone was the newspaper's "front page."

Getting the Picture

A black hole ironically pushed *The Chronicle* into color photography. Or at least, the photograph would have looked like a black hole without the color. Instead, the image of a red supernova star and its luminescent yellow ring of hydrogen gas appeared on the cover of the September 5, 1990, issue. Representing the first time such a ring had been seen by astronomers, the discovery from the Hubble Space Telescope was detailed in the *Research Notes* section inside.

Earlier, Gwaltney had made the statement that he would start using color when the *Wall Street Journal* started using color, and surely, the newspaper would never use color for a head and shoulder shot of a person. Gwaltney subsequently traveled to Hong Kong and found the Asian *Wall Street Journal*, printed with color advertisements. *The Chronicle* started accepting color advertisements upon his return. It was not long, however, before *The Chronicle* had a color photograph on almost every page, and its color printing demands were testing the capacity of its printer, which also printed *USA Today*, perhaps the pacesetter for the usage of color in daily newspapers.

The Chronicle spends thousands of dollars each week on photographs (as much as $650 per photograph). About ninety percent of them are commissioned for the newspaper and are so indicated with credit lines that include the photographer's name and "For *The Chronicle*." The remaining photographs usually are purchased from wire services. In fact, *The Chronicle* spent more than $333,000 on photographs and commissioned art for the fiscal year ended October 29, 1992.

Photography editor Rose Engelland, who marked seven years with the publication in 1993, juggles the assignments and, since the advent of the new photo "cover" design, has assumed responsibility for providing a selection of appropriately suitable cover photographs. That means earmarking at least four or five potential cover stories for each issue. Photography assignments for these articles will include two settings, a cover pose and another photograph for use on an inside page. Engelland's contacts comprise nearly four hundred photographers around the world.

"The best of all worlds is when text and photos interact," Gwaltney said (1993j). "The best picture caption, I've always maintained, is not one that says 'see the woman smiling on the right,' but a caption that makes the reader go back and look for something he or she hasn't seen on first glance."

Corbin Gwaltney, founder and editor, says he is just a "plain ol' reporter." There is no doubt, however, that he has molded the culture of The Chronicle*'s operations since the outset.*

The "Moonshooter Report," first published in 1958, served as a predecessor to The
Chronicle.

THE CHRONICLE
of Higher Education

Volume I, Number 1 — *November 23, 1966*

IVAN MASSAR, BLACK STAR

Howard W. Johnson

Politics and Higher Education: The Picture Changes for '67

Congress

By IAN E. McNETT

WASHINGTON

The 89th Congress, said President Johnson, passed more education legislation than all of its 88 predecessors combined. But with inflation, the war in Vietnam, and the results of the Congressional elections this month, the 90th Congress, convening in January, is certain to set a much slower pace.

Even this year, in the 89th's second session, the legislation affecting higher education was probably less extensive than it would have been, had Vietnam and the state of the nation's economy not exerted a dampening effect.

The 1966 Record

President Johnson was generally successful in holding the spending line in 1966.

Congress made several moves toward significant expansions of the President's higher education requests. But when all the appropriations bills had been passed, it was apparent that federal spending this fiscal year will not be substantially different from the $4.8 billion the President asked for.

The 89th Congress reduced spending for some "Great Society" programs which the President wanted, such as the National Teacher Corps. And it increased the spending for old, politically popular programs which the President wanted cut back, such as direct student loans.

Congress this year considered more than 40 bills affecting higher education, and it passed most of them. The programs it approved will affect nearly everyone on the nation's campuses—students, professors, researchers, administrators, janitors, and even animals in research laboratories.

In many cases, however, no funds were appropriated for programs that Congress authorized—"sea-grant" colleges and international education, for example. For other programs, the actual appropriations were less than the amounts authorized.

Congress continued to propel the U.S. Office of Education (USOE) from its former status as a minor fact-gathering agency to one of the six or seven biggest spenders in the U.S. Government. The legislators gave USOE $3.9 billion this year—nearly 20 per cent more than last year's $3.3 billion.

Appropriations for the National Institutes of Health (NIH) also were expanded—to $1.4 billion this year from last year's $1.2 billion.

Congress saved the life of the student loan program under the National Defense Education Act (NDEA). Mr. Johnson had proposed a rapid "phase-out" of the direct loan program, to be offset by an expansion of a newer program of guaranteed loans from private lenders. Congress ignored the President's suggestion, appropriated the full $190 million authorized for NDEA loans this year, and increased next year's authorization from $195 million to $225 million.

A $3.6 billion, three-year higher education program was approved, with nearly all the funds designated for construction of academic facilities. For the current fiscal year, $720 million was appropriated for campus building projects.

Higher education also will be affected by legislation to promote humane treatment of animals, fight poverty, control water pollution, help elementary and secondary schools, conduct water-resources research, plan for better health services, and train health technologists.

It was a good year for junior colleges. They will get 22 per cent of the funds appropriated for undergraduate facilities construction this year, 23 per cent next year, and 24 per cent the following year. Junior colleges are included in the new program to train health technologists and the old program of aid to schools which educate children of federal employees.

Next Year's Agenda

When the 89th Congress wound up its affairs, it left much unfinished business for the 90th, which will convene at noon on Jan. 10.

One item on the agenda will be modernization of the 57-year-old copyright law. A bill to revise it was approved by the House Judiciary Committee too late in the session for action this year.

A Congressional reform bill, providing for separate education committees in both houses of Congress, is likely to receive priority in the Senate.

Both houses this year passed unemployment compensation bills which would

Continued on Page 5, Column 4

California

By WILLIAM REECE

BERKELEY

Higher education was a major issue in Ronald Reagan's campaign for the governorship of California, and his decisive victory is certain to have repercussions on campuses throughout the state. Items:

►Even before the election, student rallies reminiscent of the "Free Speech Movement" of 1964-65 were occurring on the University of California's Berkeley campus. Ostensibly they were concerned with internal matters at the university, such as rules governing student conduct. But many observers thought they were prompted at least in part by a desire on the part of some groups to bring about a Berkeley-Reagan "confrontation" when, as they were sure would happen, Mr. Reagan won the election.

►Throughout his campaign, the candidate himself appeared to be doing everything possible to arrange such a confrontation after the election. In his opening speech on statewide television in September, he promised, if elected, to launch an investigation of the Berkeley campus by John J. McCone, former head of the Central Intelligence Agency and a Berkeley alumnus (class of '22). And he continued along this line throughout the election campaign.

►Among many faculty members, rumors were plentiful that if Mr. Reagan won the election, it would be only a matter of time before Clark Kerr, Cal's president, would be forced out of the university. For his part, Mr. Kerr has often said he would stay in his job at least until the university celebrated its centennial in 1968. And at a post-election press conference, when a reporter asked if the election results would change his plans, Mr. Kerr answered, "No."

►California's superintendent of public instruction, Max Rafferty, a frequent critic of Mr. Kerr and the university, was an outspoken Reagan supporter and is expected to play a large role in the new governor's administration.

►The chancellor of the University of California at Los Angeles, Franklin Murphy, is generally regarded as a favorite of the southern California members of the university board of regents, many of whom also happen to be Reagan supporters. Mr. Murphy has frequently been mentioned as a likely successor to Clark Kerr, if and when Mr. Kerr leaves the presidency.

►By virtue of his new office, Mr. Reagan will sit on both the university's board of regents and the state colleges' board of trustees. In addition, he will appoint new members to these two boards and to the state board of education as the terms of present appointees expire. The state board of education provides state-level guidance to the state's 78 public junior colleges.

Mr. Reagan's Charges

In his campaign, Mr. Reagan charged that the "New Left" was using the university campus as a propaganda base and accused Gov. Edmund G. "Pat" Brown of a policy of "appeasement" toward the institution. In the aftermath of the Free Speech Movement and subsequent troubles at Berkeley, he said, undergraduate applications have dropped, professors are leaving, and graduates are finding that employers "are leery about hiring them because of the university's new reputation for radicalism."

Asked to comment, officials at Berkeley said:

"The university is not involved in

Continued on Page 4, Column 1

New MIT President Hopes For Basic-Science 'Oases'

By HOWARD SPERGEL

CAMBRIDGE, MASS.

An antique weather vane hanging over a fireplace indicates the directions that the Massachusetts Institute of Technology will take under its new president, 44-year-old Howard Wesley Johnson.

Shortly after Mr. Johnson, his wife, and three children moved into their official residence in Cambridge last summer, he wanted to hang his horse-shaped weather vane above the mantel in the living room. Institute maintenance workers told him it could not be done. Mr. Johnson listened to the advice, got some hooks and picture wire, and put up the weather vane himself.

He Answers Some Questions

The other day, Mr. Johnson talked about his plans and concerns for the development of MIT. Here are tape-recorded highlights of the conversation.

Q. Mr. Johnson, what directions would you like to see MIT take under your administration?

A. A president can make some significant additions to a university. But I would be modest about the full effect of them. I think you have to realize that an institution like this one is on what I would call a long cycle. It moves like the tide. It has a style. It has a purpose which is very deeply set in it.

Q. Are you saying that you plan to follow and develop a direction that has been previously set?

A. Yes. There will be no right-angle turns. What you would expect to find is a continuation of some very long and deep-seated interests of the institute.

Q. What are some of these interests?

A. Well, the institute has been deeply interested in the education of people to deal with the technological society. The first range of interests relates to the ends of pure science, where you have to find answers to the fundamental questions being raised in science. The second range of interests concerns application. It includes technology, mainly, in the sense of engineering. It includes also the very important range of what I would call social ideas—relating to economics and psychology, political science, management, architecture, and city planning.

Now the whole range of concerns that MIT has had over the years is buttressed

Continued on Page 6, Column 1

Wanted: A New Institutional Grants Plan

By BARBARA E. FIELD

WASHINGTON

More than 1,000 educators urged the Federal government last week to create a new system of general institutional support.

The National Association of State Universities and Land-Grant Colleges and the Association of State Colleges and Universities urged Congress to enact a $150 million "national institutional grants program" for the support of education and research in the natural and social sciences, engineering, and mathematics—a program intended "to complement, not supplant or diminish" present special-purpose science programs.

The recommendation resulted from the first joint annual meeting of the two organizations in Washington last week. Together, the 304 member-institutions of the two associations enroll more than half of the students now attending U.S. colleges and universities.

Declaring that the recommendation was only a first step, Fred H. Harrington, president of the University of Wisconsin, commented: "We've always been interested in the art of the possible."

Mr. Harrington warned that some form of over-all institutional support will be necessary as enrollments increase and as institutions become further involved in public service. He called such support the "number one unmet need" in the government's partnership with higher education.

One university president suggested privately that deeper involvement in public service would be difficult, if not prohibitive, if general institutional support were not forthcoming.

Proposals for Congress

At the end of their joint meeting, the associations issued a common legislative program for 1967 and said: "Controversy over *how* college and university operating costs may be supported by the federal government has divided both educators and the general public. The century-old experience of the land-grant institutions and more recent adoption of the principle of operating support in certain health-related fields show that methods can be found to solve this first-priority problem."

The associations expressed a willingness to cooperate with other higher education groups to develop a formula to accomplish that purpose.

In the meantime, the associations recommended enactment of the national institutional grants program. That proposal was embodied in a bill introduced this year in the 89th Congress by Rep. George P. Miller (D-Calif.), chairman of the House Science and Astronautics Committee, but no formal hearings were held on the measure. Although the bill was not a priority item to them at the time, the two associations supported it in testimony on the geographical distribution of federal science funds before the Senate Subcommittee on Government Research.

The Miller bill is expected to reappear next year. Mr. Miller was re-elected to the 90th Congress, and in a recent letter to Fred Harcleroad, president of California State College at Hayward and president-elect of ASCU, the Congressman said he would reintroduce the measure. He asked for the association's continued "strong support" for it.

Leland Haworth, director of the Na-

Continued on Page 8, Column 2

The Chronicle *made its debut in November, 1966, when campus unrest placed one of journalism's most dramatic contemporary reporting challenges on college campuses.*

THE CHRONICLE
of Higher Education

Volume IV, Number 31   May 11, 1970

A Week of Tragedy: Disorders Flare, 4 Students Die As U.S. Action in Cambodia Inflames Many Campuses

A Kent State University coed clasps her head in anguish upon seeing the body of a fellow student who was killed when National Guardsmen fired at protesters.

By PHILIP W. SEMAS

The most violent wave of disorders in the history of the nation's campuses followed President Nixon's decision to send American combat troops into Cambodia.

Four students lay dead at Kent State University last week after National Guardsmen fired on a crowd protesting the war in Southeast Asia and the Reserve Officers Training Corps.

Because of the Kent State shootings and the action in Cambodia, thousands of students went on strike on at least 200 campuses. Some demonstrators set fires, occupied buildings, threw rocks and bottles, and battled with police.

The four students killed at Kent State were Allison Krause, a freshman; Sandra Lee Scheuer, a junior; Jeffrey Miller, a freshman; and William K. Schroeder, a sophomore. Miss Krause was described as an innocent bystander who earlier in the day had told her parents by phone that she was opposed to the demonstrations.

3 Others in Critical Condition

Three other students were seriously wounded and in critical condition. They were John Cleary, Dean Kahler, and Joseph Lewis, all freshmen. Seven other students were less seriously wounded.

The shootings came after four days of protest over a variety of issues at Kent State. The protests began with rallies on Friday, May 1, by anti-war groups and a black student group. That night a number of students went on a window-smashing rampage through downtown Kent.

Mayor Leroy Satrom of Kent then asked Ohio Gov. James A. Rhodes for assistance from the National Guard, but the troops did not arrive until the following evening. On Saturday night the students held another anti-war rally and the university's ROTC building was burned down.

On Monday the students called another anti-war rally to consider possible future action, including a strike. National Guardsmen broke up the rally with tear gas. A few students tossed tear gas canisters and rocks at the police.

Guardsmen Hemmed In

As the guardsmen chased students around the campus, some guardsmen were hemmed in by demonstrators on two sides. Several witnesses said the guardsmen turned, knelt, and fired as if following an order. The guardsmen fired into the crowd, not above it, witnesses said.

When the guardsmen knelt, several students cried out that the guardsmen would use blanks. When the guardsmen opened fire and students began to fall, the crowd ran in panic. "They didn't use blanks! They didn't use blanks!" one girl screamed.

At first, the National Guard officials claimed that the guardsmen had fired in response to shots fired by a sniper. Later they said they had been told by a police helicopter that a sniper had spotted a sniper, but police officials disputed that report. Students, reporters, university officials, and others who witnessed the shooting said they had heard no sniper fire.

National Guard officials later said that the guardsmen, fired from earlier actions in a Teamsters Union strike, had misunderstood an order to fire warning shots and fired directly into the crowd.

Col. James Simmons, military personnel officer in the Ohio adjutant general's office, said the state had a policy "that our troops will not go out for riot duty without loaded weapons." Kent State was closed after the shootings and students were told to go home. Two days later, all but 300 had left Kent. The campus was cordoned off by National Guardsmen and even faculty members were barred.

Kent State President Robert I. White summed up the feeling of the campus on the day of the deaths: "Everyone without exception...

Continued on Page 3, Column 2

Diary of a Tense Night at a Yale 'Command Post'

By WM. HAMILTON JONES

NEW HAVEN, CONN.

May 1, celebrated as Law Day in many communities, was the date selected for a massive demonstration here in support of Bobby G. Seale and other Black Panthers awaiting trial here on murder charges.

The demonstration was planned to come on the heels of a two-week student strike at Yale University that had been called, in part, to dramatize concern over whether the Panthers could receive a fair trial. Yale President Kingman Brewster, Jr., also had expressed his personal skepticism concerning "the ability of black revolutionaries to receive a fair trial anywhere in the United States."

While the demonstration turned out to be only half as large as predicted, and while rumored plans for violence never materialized,

both Yale and the New Haven community made extensive preparations to assure, in for an around-the-clock operation because it President Brewster's words, that the weekend would be "peaceful and non-violent."

Although Yale had no part in sponsoring the demonstrations, Mr. Brewster pledged that the university would be open to accommodate the many out-of-towners expected for the weekend—"to the limit of sensible and safe housing and manageable food service."

"I think the situation would have been infinitely more provocative if we had turned Yale into a closed fortress," he said later.

To handle the task of coordinating the university's plans for the weekend, Mr. Brewster put his special assistant, Henry Chauncey, Jr., in charge of an administrative team that eventually numbered over half-a-dozen people.

Mr. Chauncey began by establishing a "com-

mand center" in Yale's Alumni House, ideal for an around-the-clock operation because it contained kitchen and bedroom facilities, as well as office space.

Special telephone lines were installed, including direct lines connecting Mr. Chauncey to the chief of the New Haven police and the chief of the campus police.

In addition, telephones were installed for a 24-hour-a-day information service, where people could call to verify rumors or find answers to their questions.

From Thursday night until Sunday afternoon, Alumni House served as the central office for all administrative decisions concerned with the weekend rallies.

What follows is a partial log of activities at the center from Saturday afternoon until early Sunday morning.

3:30 A college master calls to say that many outside demonstrators are planning to stay at Yale indefinitely and that the university should make clear its policy on this. Mr. Chauncey replies that it is best to wait until Sunday, when food service returns to normal and guests have to be sponsored by a student, to see if the problem arises.

4:00 A campus policeman replaces the battery in Mr. Chauncey's radio unit.

4:15 The dean of another residential college calls to say that a National Guard unit nearby is too close to the campus. Mr. Chauncey replies: "I'm not going to be party to moving the Guard today after they performed so well yesterday. I doubt they they're doing." (All forces, including state police and the National Guard units, were under the command of City Police Chief James F. Ahern.)

4:25 The rally on the New Haven Green gets under way. Mr. Chauncey listens to WYBC, the student radio station.

5:35 A call on the campus police radio indicates a bomb scare in Hendrie Hall, a building housing undergraduate organizations.

5:45 A campus policeman radios that Hendrie Hall "checks out clean."

5:47 In response to a faculty member's call, Mr. Chauncey says he is a little uneasy about how it's going to turn out this evening."

6:30 Mr. Chauncey and Peter DeG. Jacobi, his assistant, discuss whether student groups should provide music at various locations on campus during the evening. On one hand, they do not want the music to attract those who otherwise might leave Yale following the rally. On the other hand, if large numbers of demonstrators remain, music would occupy them.

6:55 There is brief speculation about how the property damage of the weekend will affect the university's insurance costs.

6:58 After talking with the students handling plans for music in the evening, everyone agrees to play the situation by ear; if many demonstrators stay beyond dinner, music will be provided; otherwise, not.

A Black Panther pleads for time to cool the situation during a tear gas attack on a protest march in New Haven.

7:05 Word is received that the rally on the Green is breaking up.

7:15 The police radio mentions a possible disturbance on High Street, where people have congregated around a fire truck responding to a false alarm.

7:17 The Mayor's office telephones to inquire about the High Street disturbance.

7:19 The assistant chief of the campus police calls to say he has asked student marshals to break up the gathering on High Street.

7:35 An administrator calls from a residential college to say they are shutting down the dinner line there, although it was advertised that food would be available until 10 p.m. A phone call by Mr. Jacobi reopens the dinner line.

7:45 The police radio reports that a fire alarm in the law school has been pulled. A check reveals no fire.

Continued on Page 6, Column 1

Campus unrest was a major story for The Chronicle *during its early years.*

THE CHRONICLE
of Higher Education

Volume V, Number 2

October 5, 1970 · $1

'RECONCILIATION MUST BEGIN. . . .WE MUST START'

"Violence must end. Understanding must be renewed."
Above, a bullet-riddled window at Jackson State College.

The

SCRANTON
REPORT

Text of the Findings of the President's Commission on Campus Unrest

In 1970, The Chronicle *devoted an issue to the "Scranton Report," the findings of the President's Commission on Campus Unrest.*

SUMMER EDITION

THE CHRONICLE
of Higher Education

June 28, 1976 • 75¢
Volume XII, Number 16

News Summary

Articles on inside pages

Church-related colleges may be given state funds for their operating expenses, the Supreme Court said in a historic ruling last week. Story on Page 3.

Women faculty members lost ground this year in their efforts to attain equality in hiring, salaries, and academic rank, according to the American Association of University Professors' annual survey of faculty salaries. A report on the survey, including average faculty compensation at more than 1,400 institutions, appears on Pages 5-8.

The First Amendment could be used by universities to defend themselves against unwanted intrusion by the federal government, the president of Brigham Young University told more than 300 college lawyers. Story on Page 8.

A "super division" for big-time college football has been proposed by a committee of the National Collegiate Athletic Association. A story and the breakdown of the proposed new N.C.A.A. divisions appears on Page 9.

Students in South Africa demonstrated against that country's educational policies, while students in Great Britain protested a shortage of jobs for teachers. In Lebanon, classes have resumed at the American University of Beirut, despite continued fighting. Foreign news appears on Page 4.

Teachers may be fired for striking illegally, the Supreme Court has ruled in a case that could have major implications for college faculty unions. Story on Page 3.

New lobbying legislation now before Congress could present problems for some of the associations that represent colleges in Washington. Story on Page 11.

The complete text of the new federal regulations on the right of students to have access to their educational records under the Buckley Amendment appears on Pages 13 and 14.

The Democratic convention will consider several proposals from its platform committee for increasing federal support for higher education. Story on Page 11.

Summer events of interest to the academic community are listed in a special calendar appearing on Pages 20 and 21.

ALSO IN THIS ISSUE

Great Moments in Higher Education
The Chronicle's own Bicentennial history

The day Thomas Jefferson hit on his design for the University of Virginia

Illustration for The Chronicle by Cameron Gerlach

The summer of 1976 brought full-page drawings to the front page, commemorating "Great Moments in Higher Education."

THE CHRONICLE
of Higher Education

November 15, 1976 • 75¢
Volume XIII, Number 11

News Summary

Articles on inside pages

Scientific journals would be forced to label many of their articles as "advertisements" if an order from the U. S. Postal Service is not changed. Story on Page 3.

Ewald B. Nyquist, New York's controversial commissioner of education, has been told by a majority of the members of the board of regents that he should retire or face dismissal. Mr. Nyquist has postponed a decision on the request until the regents meet this week. Story on Page 5.

Tuition at many public institutions has risen sharply this year, according to a survey conducted by the National Association of State Universities and Land-Grant Colleges. Story on Page 7.

Self-paced methods of instruction can significantly improve student attitudes and performance, according to studies described at a conference on productivity in higher education. Many faculty members, however, are unenthusiastic. Story on Page 6.

The test that students will take for admission to next fall's entering class at medical schools will be harder and longer than the one administered in previous years. The new examination will be given for the first time next spring. Story on Page 12.

Bond issues affecting higher education were approved in four states and defeated in two in this month's voting. Story on Page 5.

Two Quebec universities have been virtually closed by strikes of faculty unions. The chief issues are job security and governance. Story on Page 11.

Mark Twain kept voluminous journals and notes, many of which are being published for the first time. A review of two volumes of those materials appears on Page 15.

The South's Black Colleges Lose a Football Monopoly

They alone fielded black players while segregation prevailed; now the once-lily-white institutions recruit blacks heavily

PHOTOGRAPH FOR THE CHRONICLE BY MARC PoGAL

By Larry Van Dyne

GRAMBLING, LA.

A dozen years ago the football team at Louisiana State University—its roster an unsullied white—had no room for a running back who was black, no matter how good he was. Racial mixing, as in most of the Deep South's state universities, was unthinkable.

Unless he went North, a black Louisiana running back usually played at one of the state's two predominantly black institutions—either here at Grambling College or at Southern University in Baton Rouge.

By the time Terry Robiskie, a young black runner, came out of high school in south Louisiana in 1972, however, L.S.U. had begun to make peace with integration and, at last, to notice the state's black athletes. Its coaches recruited Robiskie heavily—and won a struggle against Southern, Tulane, Notre Dame, Oklahoma, and others for his talents.

Their judgment proved correct. This fall, Robiskie is the leading rusher in the Southeastern Conference and has just become the top ground-gainer in L.S.U.'s history.

Robiskie's decision to play for a white school down home—a decision being repeated by dozens of black athletes across the South—is reflected in football rosters throughout the region this fall, some 13 years after Gov. George Wallace stood in the door at Alabama as a symbol of resistance to integration.

Change Has Been Swift

Teams in the Southeastern Conference, which stretches through the heart of the old Confederacy—from Florida and Georgia through Alabama, Tennessee, and Mississippi into Louisiana—show rosters that are roughly a third black. The same is true in the Southwest Conference, which comprises the major football powers in Arkansas and Texas.

Once the old barrier was broken, the change was striking and relatively swift. The first black football players did not appear in

Grambling State University, long a football power among black colleges, faces new competition for top black athletes from the South. For example, Terry Robiskie, below, chose to play for the once all-white Louisiana State.

J. BARRY MITTAN

the Southwest Conference until 1966 (at Southern Methodist and Baylor) or in the Southeastern Conference until 1967 (at Kentucky). Yet at one point this fall, nine of the 10 top running backs in each conference were blacks.

In the last few years Florida, Houston, Kentucky, Southern Methodist, and Tennessee all have started blacks at quarterback—that position of brains and authority that white fantasy had long deemed beyond black capabilities.

Effects on Black Colleges

While the recruiting of black athletes by white institutions is adding a new dimension to their football traditions, it is having less visible, but profound effects on the South's predominantly black colleges. This handful of small institutions, which struggled for years in the segregated setting to provide opportunities for black athletes and a rallying point for black communities, are now having to adjust to the disappearance of their old monopoly on black talent.

Some 33 of the country's 104 black colleges field football teams. Their reputation nationally rests on the remarkable large number of players they have sent on to prominence in professional football.

The fledgling American Football League, which began playing in 1960, was the first to draw large numbers of players from the black colleges. The older, rival National Football League soon joined in self-defense.

This year, some 169 of the N.F.L.'s players—about 15 per cent—came out of black colleges.

Twelve black colleges—all state-supported—had at least 816 players on N.F.L. rosters at the opening of this season. Grambling led with 19, followed by Tennessee State (18), Jackson State (13), Texas Southern (12), Alcorn State (11), Stockton (10), University of Arkansas-Pine Bluff (7), Morgan State (7), Prairie View A&M (7), Florida A&M (5).

Continued on Page 8, Column 1

Athletics became a major section in The Chronicle *in 1982.*

FORTNIGHTLY
March 7, 1980
$1

BOOKS&ARTS

FILM: Richard Gere
in 'Gigolo'

RECORDS: Rock's new
wave rolls in

RECORDS: Spain's gifted
guitar music

BOOKS: The Mauler
as metaphor

Canada's novelist-poet Margaret Atwood

Books and Arts, *a generic circulation spinoff of* The Chronicle *launched in 1979, lasted only six months. Although journalistically acclaimed, the publication was losing money at the rate of $1 million a year.*

THE CHRONICLE OF PHILANTHROPY

ISSN 1040-6762 • Copyright © 1988 by The Chronicle of Philanthropy

Vol. I, No. 1 • October 25, 1988 • $2.75

GIVING

In Charitable Giving, Volunteers Lead and the Wealthy Lag

New survey finds the poor more generous than the rich

By KRISTIN A. GOSS
WASHINGTON

Volunteers saved America's non-profit organizations at least $150-billion last year and were more than three times as generous with their dollars as people who did not volunteer, according to a study released last week.

At the same time, the study found, low-income donors and people with strong religious commitments are more likely to give a greater proportion of their salaries, and are more likely to volunteer, than are their wealthy and non-religious counterparts.

'A Stark Contrast'

"Giving and volunteering in America presents a stark contrast between heart-warming generosity and bone-chilling selfishness," said Brian O'Connell, president of Independent Sector, a national coalition of non-profit organizations and grant makers, which commissioned the survey. Mr. O'Connell said he was discouraged by the number of wealthy adults who "don't give a damn" about those less fortunate, but heartened by the philanthropic spirit of lower-income groups and by the "the clear potential for enlisting" many more people to volunteer.

The 219-page study, *Giving and Volunteering in the United States, 1988*, is
Continued on Page 8

GIVING

157 Foundations Make AIDS Grants; $51-Million Awarded

Foundation grants for programs related to acquired immune deficiency syndrome have increased dramatically in the last year.

Foundations have given $31-million for AIDS programs since August, 1987—60 per cent of the $51.6-million awarded since 1983, according to a study released last week.

In the past five years, 157 foundations have made 593 grants for AIDS programs, according to *AIDS Funding: A Guide to Giving by Foundations and Charitable Organizations*, the report of the study.

The report, by the Foundation Center, a non-profit clearinghouse that tracks grants, was based on responses from 3,200 private foundations.

The total number of foundations awarding grants for AIDS projects increased from 4 in 1983 to 157 by August 1988. And 40 of the 100 largest foundations in the United States have awarded
Continued on Page 10

THE NEWS IN BRIEF

Giving

"The most important foundation appointment in 20 years" is how one expert describes the choice of Peter Goldmark (*right*) to head the Rockefeller Foundation. In an interview, Goldmark talks about his plans for the foundation and his views on philanthropy. Story on Page 4.

Company chief executives say they are still committed to philanthropy, but misgivings about the economy make a big increase in corporate giving unlikely. In a new survey, top executives also say they want to know how gifts will contribute to their companies' goals. Story on Page 4.

"Prospect research" continues to boom. Researchers have a new national organization, and their salaries are up almost 16 per cent. "We are moving up, out of the basement," says one. Story on Page 11.

The Vatican is seeking donations to offset a $64-million debt; a new fund will offer $153-million for low-income housing; and business giving to the arts is expected to rise. Giving News in Brief: Page 5.

Management

Non-profit organizations could get millions of dollars if innovative financing ideas in a new report were adopted. Among the proposals: tax credits for businesses that make donations and postage stamps to benefit charities. Story on Page 25.

Religious broadcasters have adopted a new code of ethics that sets strict standards for accounting and fund raising. Story on Page 27.

The National Council of Churches and its relief arm, the Church World Service, are embroiled in a dispute over administrative costs. Relief officials fear the conflict could harm fund raising. Story on Page 26.

Aggressive new strategies are needed to recruit volunteers, said speakers at a meeting of people who run volunteer programs. Story on Page 29.

A former Moody Foundation official has been sentenced; Seattle Planned Parenthood has cut its ties to United Way; and a judge refused to close down P.T.L. Management News in Brief: Page 25.

Regulation

New regulations on lobbying by charities are expected soon from the I.R.S. Lobbyists expect the rules to ease many of the fears generated by the service's last batch of proposals. Story on Page 31.

Charities are confused by new I.R.S. guidance about their responsibility to disclose how much of a donor's gift is tax deductible. Story on Page 31.

Baptist churches in the South have been warned that distributing a voter-infor-mation letter could jeopardize their tax-exempt status. Story on Page 32.

Four key Congressmen have asked the I.R.S. to collect more information from non-profit organizations on their unrelated business income. Tax Watch: Page 33.

Special Report: Politics

Philanthropy's role has become a debating point in the campaign. Bush praises donors and volunteers—his "thousand points of light"—while Dukakis supporters say he has worked well with non-profit groups in Massachusetts. Story on Page 15.

Foundations are giving less for voter registration this year. Officials of get-out-the-vote groups say foundations have been scared off by controversy. But foundation officials say the drives have not been very successful. Story on Page 18.

Also in This Issue

Books	30
Coming Events	34-36
Deadlines	36
The Face of Philanthropy	2-3
Grants	12-14
Ideas	28
My View	40
People	30
Professional Opportunities	37-39
Tax Watch	33

Make-Up of Foundation Boards

White 94%
Black 4%
Hispanic 1%
Other 1%

Male 71%
Female 29%

SOURCE: COUNCIL ON FOUNDATIONS

SPECIAL REPORT

The Reagan Years: Profound Changes for Philanthropy

Shift in U.S. policies worries charities, even as gifts increase

By ANNE LOWREY BAILEY

Profound changes have taken place in American philanthropy since Ronald Reagan was elected President almost eight years ago.

► Giving to charitable causes has almost doubled, to $93.7-billion in 1987 from $48.7-billion in 1980. But the 1987 rise was only 6.5 per cent, the lowest since 1975. And corporate giving did not increase at all.

► Federal aid to non-profit organizations has been cut back or held steady, and many groups—particularly those that serve the most disadvantaged members of society—say they can barely make ends meet. But the picture is mixed: Many organizations have become more efficient, are depending less on government, and are thriving.

► Tax reform has reduced incentives for giving, but its effects are just beginning to be felt.

► Concentration of wealth in the hands of the "super rich" has led to a variety of innovative fund-raising techniques aimed at the very wealthy, from "ultimate gifts" to "prospect research."

► Competition for donations is increasing as more and more charities are conducting capital campaigns and goals are rising ever higher. More public institutions, from school systems to communities, from
Continued on Page 19

GIVING

Hospitals Try to Attract Money Usually Donated to Other Health Groups

By WENDY MELILLO
DALLAS

Launching a major campaign to double giving to their institutions by 1992, fund raisers for hospitals said they hoped to attract some of the money usually given to the United Way and health charities such as the American Cancer Society.

The $2-million campaign is needed, the fund raisers said, to forestall hospital closings and make individual donors think of hospitals when planning their charitable giving.

Speaking at the annual meeting of the National Association for Hospital Development here, Peter W. Ghiorse, vice-president for development and external affairs at St. Vincent's Hospital and Medical Center in New York, said the campaign was "a multi-media communications tool to help hospitals gain a greater share of charitable dollars. When
Continued on Page 8

The Chronicle of Philanthropy, *launched as a companion publication in 1988, became a financial success several months before its fifth anniversary.*

THE
CHRONICLE
OF HIGHER EDUCATION

August 28, 1991

Almanac

The Chronicle's Almanac *supplement includes a variety of facts and statistics concerning higher education and related political, social and economic topics.*

SPRING · SUMMER 1993

Events

IN ACADEME

THE CHRONICLE OF HIGHER EDUCATION

The Chronicle's Events *supplement includes information about meetings and convention sites.*

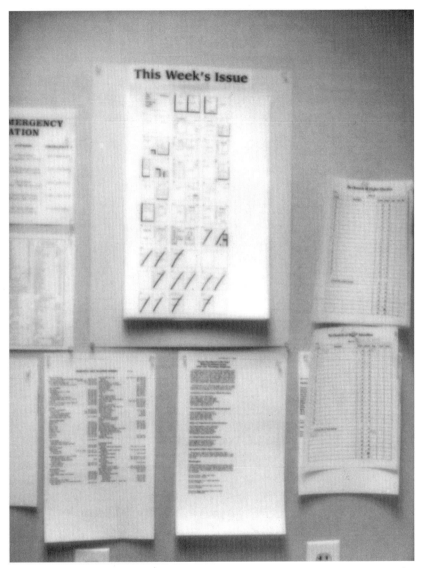

"Thursdays at the Wall." A miniature page dummy is pinned to a bulletin board on a far wall of the production area. By mid-morning, columns of set type hang from the hooks, awaiting paste-up by three production artists. A few completed dummies await final proofreading, section head approval, Malcolm Scully's initialed okay, and last, but not least, the blessing of the initials "C.G."

Deadline brings Editor Corbin Gwaltney and other staff members to the "Wall."

Managing Editor Malcolm Scully has shaped The Chronicle*'s style of synthesis reporting.*

Associate Editor Ted Weidlein has involved The Chronicle *in the "Web" and has guided the development of* "Academe this week" *on the Internet.*

Robin Ross, Associate Publisher through the early 1990s, has led The Chronicle's *advertising efforts. She compares the weekly newspaper to industry trade magazines.*

CHAPTER XI

THE BOTTOM LINE: BUSINESS DYNAMICS

Advertising

In publishing success terms, *The Chronicle* is akin to a one-news-paper town. The publication dominates its market niche, and indus-try observers have difficulty making comparisons, especially consid-ering the newspaper's profitably thick classified section.

"We think of ourselves less as a consumer publication and more as a business magazine," said Robin Ross (1993), associate publisher through the early 1990s. In terms of circulation, however, she noted the newspaper is similar to an industry trade magazine because read-ership is very concentrated in one field. In fact, in *The Chronicle*'s case, a readership survey (described below) showed that 99.7 per-cent of the publication's subscribers are employed by an institution of higher education or other organization concerned with higher education.

In comparing *The Chronicle*, in terms of advertising rates, to trade publications, Ross noted that *Advertising Age*, with a circulation of 85,000, charged $12,500 for a "junior" page, black-and-white adver-tisement. A comparable advertisement in *The Chronicle*, with more than 94,000 circulation, cost $3,600. Cost per thousand readers to-taled $38 for *The Chronicle* versus $146 for *Advertising Age*. Comparing the higher education publication to *Computerworld*, with a circulation of 137,000, the junior page rate totaled $19,000 or $112 per thousand readers. In 1993, black-and-white advertising rates in *The Chronicle* ranged from $355 for a quarter-column advertisement to $10,980 for two-page spread. Color advertising rates ranged from $5,225 for a half-page to $15,420 for a two-page spread advertisement. *The Chronicle* also offered "special category" advertising rates (black-and-white) for tax-exempt organizations, which ranged from $215 for a quarter-column to $3,440 for a tabloid page. The same rates applied to "book and journal" advertising, which also included color advertising at a cost of $2,550 per page over the basic black-and-white rate. Classified cost $70 per column inch for boxed advertisements or $1.35 per word of agate type.

According to *Advertising Age*'s June 14, 1993, "Top 300" ranking of the nation's largest magazines, *The Chronicle* ranked 208th, compared with inclusion the previous year in the top 200, at 197th place (p. S-11). The trade publication estimated *The Chronicle*'s total revenues for 1992 to be nearly $21.4 million, a 5.2 percent increase from 1991's total. Table 6 presents *The Chronicle*'s ranking information, according to the *Advertising Age* "Top 300."

TABLE 6
THE CHRONICLE OF HIGHER EDUCATION REVENUE AS RANKED BY THE ADVERTISING AGE "TOP 300"

Total revenue	$21,351
Advertising revenue	$14,138
Advertising pages	2,767
Subscriber revenue	$7,213

Note. Dollars are in thousands. Published by *Advertising Age*, June 14, 1993.

Although *The Chronicle*'s 2,767 advertising pages were down from the 2,856 listed by *Advertising Age* for 1991, the total would have placed *The Chronicle* in sixth place among the top fifteen consumer magazines by advertising pages, but the publication has not been included in the breakdown for two years as it had been for *Advertising Age*'s listings in 1990 and earlier. According to the *Advertising Age* listing, the top five consumer magazines, by annual advertising pages, were: *Hemmings Motor News* (9,534); *Forbes* (3,764); *Business Week* (3,585); *People* (3,280); and *Bride's & Your New Home*, (3,000).

In a similar ranking of all U.S. magazines on September 15, 1993, by *Folio* magazine, *The Chronicle* was listed as 198th, with its revenue estimated at $21.0 million. Leading the *Folio* list, by annual advertising pages, were: *Computer Shopper* (8,679); *PC Magazine* (7,285); *Computer Reseller News* (6,491); *PC Week* (5,580), and *PC Sources* (5,078) (McDougall, 1993).

Table 7 illustrates the ratio of news to advertising for *The Chronicle*'s recent history.

TABLE 7
THE CHRONICLE OF HIGHER EDUCATION NEWS
AND ADVERTISING RATIOS, 1988-1992

Issue	Pages	News	Advertising
November 2, 1988	103	34.00%	66.00%
November 1, 1989	128	30.00	70.00
November 7, 1990	120	31.00	69.00
November 6, 1991	120	37.26	62.74
November 4, 1992	112	35.55	64.45

Source: *The Chronicle of Higher Education.*

Note: Issues selected are the first editions of the publication's November-October fiscal years.

Circulation

Editor Gwaltney does not ask readers of *The Chronicle* what they want. He finds no incongruity in the publication's regular surveying of readers and his reluctance to "follow" readers. Thus, the introduction to a circulation letter, mailed in mid- and late summer 1992 was appropriate, "We hesitate to ask this favor, but . . ." The letter said that a number of advertisers and prospective advertisers had asked how readers use *The Chronicle*'s news, opinion, and advertising columns. Ross indicated the sales staff would like to provide "specific answers from some specific people." The letter was, plainly, a request for testimonials for use in a sales booklet. The readers obliged. The following are excepts from the letters.

1. From Donna Lopiano, executive director, Women's Sports Foundation (letter undated):

> *The Chronicle of Higher Education* is the most respected publication about our colleges and universities in the nation. More important, *The Chronicle*'s breadth of coverage is simply invaluable, from trends to legislation to conferences to employment and so many other areas, it is the single most comprehensive 'sourcebook' on higher education.

2. From Thomas J. Hayes, director of institutional advancement and chair and professor of marketing, Xavier University, Cincinnati, Ohio (letter dated August 19, 1992):

> By watching the announcements of job openings, one can gauge the mood of college campuses. The types of positions open give an indication on what administrations deem important (e.g. Emory's recent announcement for a Director of Gay and Lesbian issues).

3. From Annabelle C. Fong, director of the Financial Aid Office at the University of Hawaii at Manoa, Honolulu, Hawaii (letter dated September 23, 1992):

> I would describe *The Chronicle* as THE newspaper for whatever is happening in higher education in the nation and abroad. I've come to rely upon getting the latest news in trends, laws, events, concerns in states, athletics, etc. from *The Chronicle*, enjoying even *Marginalia* (we all need some

humor in our lives) and *In Brief*. The *Point of View* is always worth reading.

4. From Gene L. Woodruff, dean and vice provost, the Graduate School, University of Washington, Seattle, Washington (letter dated August 26, 1992):

> *The Chronicle* is the higher education community's *New York Times*. It is both the forum for discussion, and the source of the latest information for topics of importance to faculty and administrators in colleges and universities all over the U.S. I read every issue—scanning all the article titles, scanning most of the articles, and reading carefully a dozen or so articles of special interest to me. Articles from *The Chronicle* are frequently the topic of discussion at the weekly meeting of the President's Cabinet on this campus.

5. From Narcisa A. Polonio, president, Harcum Junior College, Bryn Mawr, Pennsylvania (letter dated September 8, 1992):

> If you want to see how funding for higher education compared to other departments, *The Chronicle* is the source for this information.

6. From Charles E. Cannon, chairperson, Department of Science and Mathematics, Columbia College Chicago, Chicago, Illinois (letter dated August 19, 1992):

> Usually, there is valuable information about educational software that I find very useful.

7. From Jack L. Stark, president, Claremont McKenna College, Claremont, California (letter dated August 19, 1992):

> *The Chronicle of Higher Education* is to educational leaders what the *Wall Street Journal* is to business leaders.

8. From John Straw, archivist for student life and culture, University Archives, University of Illinois at Urbana-Champaign, Illinois (letter dated September 18, 1992):

> I cannot fail to mention my personal use of *The Chronicle*. It was through a classified advertisement in *The Chronicle* that I first became aware of the challenging and interesting position that I now hold.

9. From Harold D. Germer, president, Ottawa University, Ottawa, Ontario, Canada (letter dated August 27, 1992):

> I keep the annual *Almanac* section of *The Chronicle* near at hand throughout the year.

10. From Karl J. Valentine, director of development and alumni relations, Community College of Philadelphia, Pennsylvania (letter dated August 17, 1992):

> If you value your career, keep abreast of the news in *The Chronicle*. Academia is rife with public relations facades that can only be exposed by good investigative journalism. *The Chronicle* never holds back and always gets the story straight the first time. I recommend *The Chronicle* to anyone who embarks on a career in higher education. There is no equal.

The individual voices, only 5,000 at *The Chronicle*'s launch, surpassed 50,000 in 1976 and continued growing to 97,074 for the six months ending June 30, 1993, as indicated by Table 8.

TABLE 8
THE CHRONICLE OF HIGHER EDUCATION'S
SIX-MONTH AVERAGE PAID CIRCULATION, 1967-1993

Date	Circulation	Date	Circulation
		September, 1967	8,555**
		September, 1968	12,673**
		October, 1969	17,573**
		December, 1970	20,524*
June, 1971	23,096	December, 1971	24,438
June, 1972	24,644	December ,1972	24,703
June, 1973	25,867	December, 1973	28,102
June, 1974	30,794	December, 1974	35,857
June, 1975	41,879	December, 1975	44,250
June, 1976	49,523	December, 1976	53,061
June, 1977	57,966	December, 1977	60,488
June, 1978	65,804	December, 1978	65,113
June, 1979	68,020	December, 1979	68,165
June, 1980	70,023	December, 1980	68,699
June, 1981	67,871	December, 1981	66,759
June, 1982	69,659	December, 1982	70,193
June, 1983	71,748	December, 1983	70,712
June, 1984	71,047	December, 1984	70,839
June, 1985	71,162	December, 1985	73,226
June, 1986	75,779	December, 1986	76,053
June, 1987	77,116	December, 1987	79,053
June, 1988	81,383	December, 1988	82,328
June, 1989	83,610	December, 1989	84,208
June, 1990	86,595	December, 1990	88,598
June, 1991	89,622	December, 1991	91,725
June, 1992	94,658	December, 1992	96,177
June, 1993	97,074		

Source: The Audit Bureau of Circulations.

Note: **From Statements of Ownership. *The Chronicle's* first Publisher's Statement from the Audit Bureau of Circulations.

In 1993, the publication also promised advertisers a "bonus circulation of 19,000 additional higher education professionals through distribution of the newspaper at twelve higher education conferences during the first quarter.

In early 1992, Simmons Market Research Bureau Inc. conducted a survey of *The Chronicle*'s subscribers. The study's results provided a unique look at *The Chronicle*'s readers. For example, they are all employed. They are, not surprisingly, exceptionally well educated. Their household incomes are far above average. At $75 per year for subscriptions, they are loyal. More than twenty percent of *The Chronicle*'s subscribers have been subscribing for ten years or more. Nearly fifty-three percent said they have discussed or referred an advertisement to someone else. Table 9 further illustrates the reader profile.

TABLE 9
PROFILE OF SUBSCRIBERS TO
THE CHRONICLE OF HIGHER EDUCATION

Male	66.3%
Female	33.7%
Median age	47.2 years
Masters degree or more	88.9%
Doctoral degree	51.8%
Average household income	$86,000
Own residence	77.3%
Average residence value	$192,600

Note. Source is survey conducted by Simmons Market Research Bureau Inc., 1992

In its effort to reach as many higher education constituents as possible, *The Chronicle* has attempted, even as it has grown, to keep its subscription price affordable, especially in comparison to higher education specialty newsletters and journals. The newspaper has published from twenty-two to forty-nine issues per year during its history and has charged from $10 to $75 for its subscriptions. Single copy prices have ranged from $0.60 in 1971, the first year the publication had a cover price, to $3.25 in 1993. Table 10 shows the growth of both the issues published year and the corresponding subscription price.

TABLE 10
THE CHRONICLE OF HIGHER EDUCATION
SUBSCRIPTION RATES

Year	Issues per Year	Yearly subscription price
1967	22	$10.00
1970	38	15.00
1975	42	20.00
1980	46	25.00
1985	48	48.00
1990	49	57.50
1993	49	75.00

Source: *The Chronicle of Higher Education.*

Promotion

P. T. Barnum he is not. Perhaps it is the publication's roots in foundation funds that makes Gwaltney more comfortable in his "Editor's hat," than his "Owner's cap." Or that fact he yearned from his youth to be a journalist, never a business manager. He pays consultants who tell him to be more aggressive from a business standpoint, but follows his own instincts about how a publishing business should be run. He forbids advertising sales people to negotiate "off the rate card," or, in other words, make deals other than for the published prices. He adamantly opposes the publication of "advertorials," advertising sections that appear to be editorial in nature. He does not believe in subscription incentives. He does not shrink the "news hole," or the space devoted to editorial content, to accommodate advertising. And he steadfastly does not consider a group's expenditures with the publication when assigning or editing stories, such as in the case of the Teachers Insurance and Annuity Association (TIAA), one of the largest and longest-running advertisers as well as a group that has been covered aggressively by the news side of the operation.

Thus, despite financial success, *The Chronicle* still poses unfamiliar territory for many potential advertisers and subscribers. The sales staff first has to sell the concept of higher education as a market similar to retailing or finance. To aid this effort, *The Chronicle* hired National Video Industries Inc. in New York in mid-1993 to produce its first-ever video promotion. The tape was tailored for use at sales meetings with individual advertisers, as well as at convention trade shows where *The Chronicle* frequently has booths. At an investment of about $20,000, the videotape represents one of the more pro-active self-promotions undertaken by *The Chronicle*. Gwaltney reserved judgment as to whether or not the video will provide the desired "opening wedge" to new categories of advertisers, such as issues advertising and corporate image advertising, but pledged to update the production every couple of years if it increases sales.

CHAPTER XII

THE NEXT DEADLINE:
INTERNATIONAL DEADLINES

Worldwide Coverage

Corbin Gwaltney scribbled the contract with Brian MacArthur of the *London Times Higher Education Supplement* on a cocktail napkin in a Greek Street restaurant in London's Soho area. Even before this 1971 agreement for the exchange of stories between the two publications, *The Chronicle* editor had considered the world his newspaper's beat. The coldest of cold wars could not cool his enthusiasm for delivering an international look at higher education. From the first stories resulting from the agreement, in the October 26, 1971, issue, the subsequently evolving *International* section has been responsible for some of *The Chronicle*'s most aggressive reporting efforts, with Scully directing the section through its development stages.

With its network of about twenty-five foreign correspondents, *The Chronicle* has published firsthand reports of such major international events as China's pro-democracy movement (Jacobson, 1989, p. A34), Kuwait's troubled higher education system (Thornborough, 1990, p. A27), and the toppling of Mikhail Gorbachev and the power structure of the former Soviet Union (After, 1991, p. A54). The news has been peppered with analysis and perspective, such as the publication's assessment that "stakes are high, political activity is low" on

Israel's campuses (Watzman, 1978, p. 3). Or its look at the troubled conditions of universities in Peru, home of the hemisphere's oldest university, San Marcos University in Lima (Lane, 1985, p. 85).

One of *The Chronicle*'s most exhaustive international undertakings was a special report on higher education under apartheid in South Africa, published June 11, 1986, and written by Scully and writer Paul Desruisseaux in collaboration with the newspaper's Cape Town correspondent, Helen Zille. To produce the twenty-page, 36,000-word report (Desruisseaux, Scully and Zille, 1986, p. 1–20), the writers traveled throughout South Africa, visited ten university campuses and interviewed more than 150 people. The piece outlined various ways that the country's universities were struggling to serve a society undergoing political changes and to face challenges that the country's leaders acknowledged were the most difficult in history. The report ended with a less-than-hopeful conclusion by one of the South African interviewees: "'The government says it is committed to equal education for blacks, but we say it isn't,' says Ken M. Andrew, spokesman on black education for the opposition Progressive Federal Party. 'When apartheid and equal education conflict, the government chooses apartheid'" (Desruisseaux, Scully and Zille, 1986, p. 20).

Desruisseaux, who joined *The Chronicle* in January 1982, served intermittently as an international reporter while handling other assignments for nearly a decade. He became editor of the *International* section in 1991. Desruisseaux's international assignments have been among the most dangerous undertaken by *The Chronicle*. He went to Beirut in August 1982 during the Israeli siege of the Lebanon capital, a time when the American University had been forced to cancel summer school (American, 1982, p. 29) because of the violence. He also covered the aftermath of the Salvadoran army's ransacking of the National University of El Salvador in 1983 (Desruisseaux, p. 27).

"In a lot of ways, the stories we get from overseas are more directly connected to the politics of the nation than [the stories] here," Desruisseaux said (1992). "We deal not so much with coverage of an individual institution, but take a larger approach to higher education—or rebuilding higher education."

There also have been attempts to prepare students and faculty for overseas experiences. In late 1992, while attending a meeting of the Council on International Educational Exchange in Berlin, Desruisseaux heard a panel discussion that included a young black woman who spoke frankly of her experiences. He followed up with a piece on the American black student's personal travails as a "stranger in a strange land" (For Minority, 1992, A27). One thing she had not gotten used to was what she called the "brush by," or how strangers would discreetly touch her distinctively thick and curly dark hair. She learned that many people in Berlin had never met a black person.

As well as reporting on the battle for free speech throughout the international community, *The Chronicle* has been, at times, a part of the story. Vera Rich, who covered events in Eastern Europe, was detained briefly in March 1985 and searched by Polish authorities as she prepared to leave for London. They confiscated tape recordings of interviews as well as some of her background material (*Chronicle*, 1985, p. 35).

The Chronicle further interprets its international mission as two-way by reporting activities of foreign students at American colleges and universities. For example, a 1975 front-page article reported efforts by United States colleges to recruit foreign students that resulted in increasing enrollments by 30,000 in five years (Semas, 1975, p. 1). The newspaper also examined the backlash of lost sympathy for Iranian students in the United States after so many campus demonstrations were staged that as one student said, "You get to a point where you holler so loud, no one hears you anymore" (Middleton, 1978, p. 9).

International Editions?

The international coverage and resulting opportunities have put a mark of sophistication on *The Chronicle* that did not exist during its first decade. Gwaltney attributed the newspaper's expanding capabilities to the development of depth within its staff.

"In the early days, we were just trying to put out an eight or twelve-page newspaper. So a reporter one week would be an 'expert' on one thing. The following week, he or she would be an expert on something else," the editor said (Gwaltney, 1993e). "At our annual editorial department retreats, the principal desire expressed by reporters and editors was more time. We'd say some day, maybe we'll make some money and do that."

Some day did arrive for *The Chronicle* and its international extensions developed. More time for stories and travel created a self-fulfilling prophecy. With more time, reporters gained more insight and honed their expertise in specific beat areas.

With the advent of the electronic distribution network the Internet, international growth opportunities abound for *The Chronicle*. Discussions have considered streamlined overseas editions of *The Chronicle*, facsimile versions of *The Chronicle* sent to various parts of the world, regional editions for Asia, and other ideas.

Gwaltney has some reservations, however, when it comes to language translations of *Chronicle* pieces. "We've always rejected it on the grounds that English is the lingua franca of academe wherever you go, even in China," he said (Gwaltney, 1993e). "It seems almost unnecessary to do it. As an editor, I don't know quite how I could sleep at night not being able to read the twist somebody put on the story in the course of translating it."

CHAPTER XIII

THE NEW TECHNOLOGY: THE CHRONICLE ON-LINE

Electronic/Multi-media

editor@chronicle.merit.edu

In technology terms, this is *The Chronicle*'s address on the Internet. Starting on April 13, 1993, the newspaper began providing *Academe This Week* to this network of computer networks, part of many campus networks, five informational elements based on the current week's issue. The elements included a guide to the news in the current week's issue, a calendar of the week's events in academe, a schedule of the week's Congressional hearings, the week's "deadlines" for fellowships, grant applications, exchange programs, and other programs, and a listing of job openings from *Bulletin Board*. Plans to expand the service are ongoing.

The first week, nearly 9,300 individual users used the service, making some 50,500 searches and retrieving 32,000 separate files. These users of *Academe This Week* were from Australia, Austria, Belgium, Canada, Denmark, Finland, several countries of the former Soviet Union (the Commonwealth of Independent States), Germany, Hong Kong, India, Israel, Mexico, Italy, Norway, Sweden, Switzerland, Japan, Taiwan, Venezuela, the United Kingdom, and the United States.

"Internet is becoming an international way for scholars to keep in touch with one another," Gwaltney suggested (1992k). "The wiring of campuses is, again, an historic change. Back in the mid-1980s when we began to become aware that the computer was not just another printing press, we began covering technology more and more. In 1990, we set up a separate section for it, but we're finding that technology is breaking out of its section and appearing in the scholarship or government or politics sections."

The editors also point out that the Internet affects the way people interrelate because there is not an overriding hierarchy. Indeed, Gwaltney added, just look at the photos in *The Chronicle*. Everyone seems to want to pose in front of his or her computer. The computer, he noted, is the instrument that everyone uses, from the Latin classicist to the scientist.

New Conversations

The expanded horizons have prompted new conversations in *The Chronicle*'s halls. Gwaltney has been studying the launch of a CD-ROM version of the newspaper. *The Chronicle of Philanthropy* launched in 1993 a "ChronicleFax" service that allows readers to order, via facsimile machine, a variety of articles that have been published. The service, available twenty-four hours a day, seven days a week, will be expanded to include *The Chronicle of Higher Education*. For any newspaper operation, technology can not be ignored.

"You could wake up one morning and find yourself in the category of a blacksmith shop," Gwaltney observed (1993i). "We have talked about this for years."

In fact, the Internet is not *The Chronicle*'s first interface with changing technologies. As the 1990s were getting under way, Ted Weidlein attended a meeting of university computer center directors in Snowmass, Colorado. In particular, he met with Peter Lyman, director of the Center for Scholarly Technology at the University of Southern California. The university was seeking information for its fairly sophisticated campus network. *The Chronicle*, of course, had information. The meeting resulted in a meeting of minds. Using the University of Southern California network as its so-called beta, or experimental, site, *The Chronicle* has been experimenting with the ability to distribute its full text on a university-wide system and has been slowly theorizing what information distribution channels it might pursue over the next decade.

"People use electronic media for many reasons," Weidlein said. "Some use it as an adjunct to the newspaper they actually receive. Some use it as a reference tool to find things they remember. Others are doing research or looking for particular information, like a grants list" (Weidlein, 1993k).

Weidlein continued, "We need to think in several different planes of time. The next several years is one. Over the course of five to ten years, we're trying to theorize what the possibilities will be. Our theory—and it is a shifting theory—is that we can begin to make some things available to people to build a habit of using electronic media."

"There are so many decisions to decide about our next steps electronically," noted Scully (1993k). The editors say they are willing to look at all possibilities. They noted with interest the news that the Public Broadcasting Service had plans to set up a twenty-four-hour cable channel. They say they have talked off and on for years about developing a *Meet the Press* or *60 Minutes* formatted television program on higher education. And they used *The Chronicle of Philanthropy* to test a fax service to deliver requested articles.

In addition to information dissemination, however, *The Chronicle*'s editors must also consider the place of advertisers within the electronic environment. How can they preserve the newspaper's sources of revenue? The conclusion at *The Chronicle* is that, in the short term, electronics will not replace the newsprint medium. But as Weidlein noted, "Who is to say what will happen in ten years?"

CHAPTER XIV

THE GWALTNEY LEGACY: A 'PLAIN OL' REPORTER'

Low Profile, High Impact

Gwaltney says he is just a "plain ol' reporter" (Baldwin, 1992, 1F), one of the explanations for the fact that the title of "publisher" remained unfilled some years after partner Jack Crowl retired to Vermont in 1990 for health reasons. Perhaps a more compelling reason for the longtime absence of a publisher's post within the organization is Gwaltney's carefully guarded external low profile. The septuagenarian editor quit giving speeches in the early 1980s, takes care to keep an arms-length relationship with any institution *The Chronicle* might cover, and refuses all offers of recognition, except such journalistic honors as the prestigious George Polk Award, which *The Chronicle* received in 1979 for "knowledgeable and thorough coverage of college administration in the United States" (McBee, 1979, p. A20). Even the gardens at his weekend home on the shore of Chesapeake Bay remained anonymous when featured by the *New York Times* in the spring of 1993 (Herbst, 1993, p. C1). Gwaltney simply says he is a "minimalist" (1993l).

Inside *The Chronicle*'s offices, however, there is no doubt that key decisions require the participation of *The Chronicle*'s editor and majority owner. These decisions are likely to be made over morning coffee around Gwaltney's comfortably furnished office sitting area. Internally, *The Chronicle*'s content and business directions are unquestioned as reflections of the only editor the newspaper has had in its twenty-seven-year history. Externally, the newspaper's readers simply keep weekly vigilance for the arrival of the bulky newsprint product that has become a journalistic habit within the higher education community.

"So Like Corbin"

A newspaper career was always Gwaltney's goal. He attended Johns Hopkins University because the university was a fifteen minute walk from his Baltimore home and provided the most economically feasible route to a bachelor of arts in political science. After graduation in 1943, Gwaltney served in the Army during World War II. He was captured by the Germans on December 16, 1944, the first day of the Battle of the Bulge, which history recorded as the Germans' last great offensive. He spent the rest of the war in various prison camps, an experience he termed "instructive" (Gwaltney, 1993l) in learning about starvation and one he credits for his prematurely white hair.

Upon his return to the States, Gwaltney planned to go to graduate school. Instead, he got married and went to work for Western Electric and later General Electric in industrial relations where, among other things, he edited a company magazine. His wife, who worked at the Johns Hopkins alumni office, mentioned that the administration was dissatisfied with the alumni publication—composed largely of class notes. Gwaltney spent $100, what he considered a great expense at the time, to produce a prototype of a new publication. He sent it to the provost, a former *Baltimore Sun* executive. The two had an immediate rapport, and soon Gwaltney was on an airplane to New York to talk to alumni and publishers. His magazine career had begun in earnest.

With *Life* magazine as his benchmark, Gwaltney turned the Johns Hopkins magazine into an award-winning model for alumni publications. But after about nine years, he yearned to apply the same content and design techniques to higher education in general. Thus came his *Moonshooter* days, and *The Chronicle*.

He never worried about the risks. In fact, the editor seemed to savor them, remembering the many dinnertime conversations as a child when his father, who came from poverty, would speak of the importance of security.

"I got very contemptuous of the idea of everything for security," Gwaltney said (1993l). "I decided I was never going to be like my father."

Now, with security assured with *The Chronicle*'s success, wordsmith Gwaltney does not seem acquainted with the term "retirement." While it may have been a possibility, although perhaps still not a probability, before his second wife died in August 1990, Gwaltney leads the newspaper into its second quarter-century with no acknowledgement whatsoever of retirement. Just as he sketches page layouts every week, he continues to make his Corbin-esque mark on *The Chronicle*. "So like Corbin" is a familiar phrase around *The Chronicle*'s office.

For example, it was "so like Corbin" to load the entire staff onto a double-decker bus after the deadline for the newspaper's twentieth anniversary issue for a surprise party at Washington's posh Willard Hotel. It was "so like Corbin" to take the staff's gift to him on the twenty-fifth anniversary—a wall hanging showing each staff member's year of arrival—make it into a poster, and give it back to the staff. It was "so like Corbin" to throw a fifth anniversary party for *The Chronicle of Philanthropy* (inviting the staffs from both *Chronicles*) at Nora's, a popular Washington restaurant frequented by the President and Vice President. It also was "so like Corbin" to tear up a page at 4:30 P.M. on deadline day in order to include a story discussing the higher education aspect of a bill passed by Congress late in the day.

The strategic actions are as important internally—for morale reasons, Gwaltney said, as for the external results. "Everybody here is challenging everybody else all the time," he said. "It's a kind of place where there's a feeling . . ." (Gwaltney, 1993l). Others use the word "culture."

Cultural Diversity

In fact, *The Chronicle*'s organizational culture, at least some visible parts of it, is on display. A wall in one of the office's coffee/

kitchen areas is dedicated to what Gwaltney calls an "assemblage," although official office paperwork terms it the "One Thousandth Issue Collage."

The contributions to the wall collage ran the gamut of items, reflecting emotions and representing milestones for *The Chronicle* and often higher education. All illustrate the camaraderie of *The Chronicle*'s staff. A list of the items is posted nearby for identification. For example, office manager Lisa Birchard contributed an interior decorator's card with fabric swatch "that CG said 'looks like a cheap suit.'"

The display advertising department reproduced an insertion order from "The Advocate: Ad Agency From Hell." Then sports editor Doug Lederman gave a button from Southern Methodist University's first homecoming without football. Writer Scott Heller contributed a *New York Times Magazine* cover story "chasing after our (my) coverage of the challenges to the literary canon mounted in English departments like that of Duke University."

His Weekly Window on the World

Although readers have very little personal knowledge of the man behind the *Marginalia* initials "C. G.," the weekly humor column has provided Gwaltney's singular first-person voice to *The Chronicle*'s pages since December 1, 1975. Gwaltney explained the space, which is the only place a human being, in the form of "we," addresses the reader.

"Marginalia was born of my belief that it never hurts any publication to let a human touch show through," Gwaltney said (Gwaltney, 1993d). "And since we have no editorial page, we had no place to use the first person plural pronoun."

Typically illustrative of Gwaltney's humor is the item in the September 7, 1994, *Marginalia* column:

> We've received the following from *International Who's Who*, a publication whose letterhead identifies it as "The Ultimate Professional Directory:"
> 'Dear Chronicle Hghr Educ,
> As the result of recent studies of millions of professionals, you have been selected as a potentially qualified candidate

for inclusion in the 1994 edition of *International Who's Who.*

Specifically, Chronicle Hghr Educ, our researchers gather information from numerous available sources including professional associations and societies, trade organizations, newspapers and magazines, professional reference publications and anonymous referrals from existing members. . . . .

Recognition of this kind is a heritage shared by thousands of unique professionals for over 100 years. The publication is also a tremendous networking tool and third party endorsement.

As a highly respected professional in your field, we believe your achievements merit very serious consideration for inclusion . . . .'

Chronicle Hghr Educ is speechless.

The column idea started somewhat as a collection of mini essays, ending with a few "wisecracks," as Gwaltney described the comments. Over time, however, with the help of readers' contributions, the column has become the depository of spoofs and bloopers that other people commit in student newspapers, faculty memos and other such communiques.

From time to time and from season to season, the format of *Marginalia* may change. Sometimes, Gwaltney has let photos deliver the message, such as the issue that featured pictures from the University of Miami school of medicine yearbook (*Marginalia*, 1978, p. 2). The yearbook editor, borrowing an idea from *The Jump Book*, had gotten various university officials, including the president, to be photographed in various stages of jumping.

During the summer of 1978, Gwaltney used the space for a bumper sticker contest. Reader submissions varied from "Honk if You're an Elitist" to "College Helps—To Some Degree" to "Teachers Have Class." For Gwaltney, the gambit was a "wonderful idea. You get the summer off. The readers are doing the work for you."

Every Christmas, Gwaltney does the work for the readers, by composing a holiday poem. In 1986 (*Marginalia*, p. 2) the piece began:

Again we take our Penn in hand
(If we don't some pettifogger'll)
And send from here throughout the land
Our annual year-end doggerel:

The verse that followed continued the play on university names and holiday sayings.

A drawer in Gwaltney's desk is stuffed with *Marginalia* submissions. About six to seven of the thirty to thirty-five weekly mailings are selected for use. "I do get a lot of mail for the column," Gwaltney acknowledged. "Some are quite funny. Some are sort of . . . marginal."

The Next Generation

Some months after Crowl's retirement in 1990 for health reasons, Gwaltney bought his partner's ownership interest and became sole owner of *The Chronicle*. In 1992, Gwaltney initiated an arrangement to share ownership with members of top management. He is adamant that control continue with those he has hand-picked, but recognizes the situation to be the typical classic small business problem of how to pass the business from one generation to the next. He has put in place a structure whereby the top management have become minority owners in the company.

Gwaltney says he is not concerned about cashing out his own investment. Almost no decision at *The Chronicle* is made on the basis of economics, although the editor is quite cognizant of the privileges of success: "When higher education was under fire, Harvard University sailed above everyone else. This was possible only because they were well off. The same is true of a newspaper" (Gwaltney, 1993l).

Former partner Crowl remembered that the two journalists got lectures from lawyers when they were buying the newspaper. The advice: There are only two stockholders. To make things work, they would have to respect the other's opinions.

"We nodded our heads," Crowl said (1993). "We both had some misgivings and trepidations, I guess. As far as I'm concerned, it always worked out very well."

Crowl said the operation did not change much after the buyout. In fact, without a board of directors to report to, they just had a short walk down the hall when decisions had to be made.

"We were the board," Crowl said (1993). "We had nobody else to worry about."

Crowl said the two found they had complementary strengths. He was a word person. Gwaltney was the visual constituent. While Gwaltney was prone to yield to a mercurial temperament; Crowl was the center of office calm. Gwaltney concentrated on the editorial side; Crowl was flexible enough to manage the business side.

"The whole time we worked together I don't think we ever had a really substantive disagreement on issues that we were unalterably opposed to one another," Crowl said (1993). "Of course, we had squabbles. Everybody does. But we never had a substantive disagreement on a major issue. I assume that's unusual. He's the only business partner I've ever had so I have nothing to compare."

They both had high standards, but Gwaltney was "virtually uncompromising," Crowl said, a fact that motivated him—and still motivates others—to greater accomplishments.

Gwaltney may be just a "plain ol' reporter," but he is one with a legacy for future journalists and leaders in higher education.

APPENDIX A

HISTORICAL TIME LINE

Highlights In *The Chronicle's* **History**

November 23, 1966. Volume I, Number 1. Number of pages in issue: 8. Number of full-time staff members: 12. Paid circulation: 5,000. Subscription price: $10 per year.

July 12, 1967. First twelve-page issue.

September 29, 1969. Weekly publication begins.

March 23, 1970. First classified advertisements published: 3 "Positions Available."

May 1, 1970. Offices moved from Baltimore to 1717 Massachusetts Avenue, N.W. Lead story: "A week of tragedy: Disorders flare, 4 students die as U.S. action in Cambodia inflames many campuses."

September 28, 1970. First display advertising published: one-half page from Jossey-Bass, plus two smaller advertisements.

October 5, 1970. Special issue devoted to "Scranton Report," the findings of President's Commission on Campus Unrest. Number of pages: 24, in two sections. Number of staff members: 19. Circulation: 20,500.

February 22, 1971. First best-seller list, "What They're Reading on Campuses" (No. 1: *Love Story* by Erich Segal). Single copy price: 50 cents.

October 18, 1971. First *Point of View* article: "The debasement of liberal education," by Morris B. Abram. Number of pages: 8. Number of staff members: 20. Circulation: 24,500.

October 26, 1971. First full page of international news.

January 31, 1972. *Bulletin Board* advertisements fill entire page for first time.

May 30, 1972. Special issue: "Higher Education and the Black American: Phase II." Number of pages: 12. Number of staff members: 21. Circulation: 24,500.

May 12, 1973. Biggest issue to date: 28 pages, including text of Newman report on graduate education.

November 3, 1975. First use of Atex to set live editorial matter (for *Point of View* page only).

November 10, 1975. First *Marginalia* column. Number of pages: 24. Number of staff members: 24. Circulation: 44,000.

January 12, 1976. First issue with 40 pages. Single copy price: 75 cents.

May 24, 1976. Last issue using any hot-metal composition. Number of pages: 40. Number of staff members: 28. Circulation: 49,500.

September 18, 1978. First issue of *Chronicle Review* supplement (later called *Books & Arts*). Number of pages: 72 (including 32 for *Review*). Number of staff members: 43. Circulation: 65,000.

November 1978. Corbin Gwaltney and John A. Crowl acquire *The Chronicle* from Editorial Projects for Education.

January 29, 1979. Offices moved to 1333 New Hampshire Avenue, N.W. Number of pages: 40. Number of staff members: 45. Circulation: 65,000.

February 5, 1979. *The Chronicle* receives George Polk Award for education reporting.

September 14, 1979. *Chronicle Review* spun-off to *Books & Arts*. Featured an interview with author Tom Wolfe, "the man who brought us 'radical chic.'"

March 7, 1980. Last issue of *Books & Arts*.

September 2, 1981. *Bulletin Board* reaches 31 pages. Single copy price: $1.25.

January 13, 1982. *Chronicle* Type & Design established. Number of pages: 64. Number of staff members: 60. Circulation: 67,000.

September 1, 1982. *Athletics* section created. Lead article: "Colleges urged to teach athletes, coaches the dangers of drug abuse and 'doping.'"

December 12, 1984. Offices moved to 1255 23rd Street, N.W. Number of pages: 96. Number of staff members: 75. Circulation: 70,000. Single copy price: $1.75.

September 4, 1985. 1985-86 Back to School issue. Number of pages: 160. Number of staff members: 86. Circulation: 72,000. Pages of classified advertising: 45.75. Pages of display advertising: 46.08.

June 11, 1986. Special report on South Africa.

September 3, 1986. 1986-87 Back to School issue. Number of pages: 192. Number of staff members: 90. Circulation: 78,000. Pages of classified advertising: 56. Pages of display advertising: 51. Single copy price: $1.95.

November 20, 1986. Twentieth anniversary issue.

September 2, 1987. Section 2 becomes a pull-out section. Circulation: 79,000.

October 28, 1987. *End Paper* debuts with "Wordsworth: Intimations of his immortality."

October 1988. First issue of *The Chronicle of Philanthropy*. Number of editorial staff members: 14. Circulation: 10,000.

November 20, 1991. Twenty-fifth anniversary issue. Circulation: 91,000.

June 24, 1992. First issue with current "magazine-style" cover design. Circulation: 94,000.

January 1993. Expansion of offices at 1255 23rd St. N.W. to 32,000 square feet.

February 24, 1993. *Notes from Academe* started as bi-weekly feature: "A concert honors an unforgettable mural of Black achievement."

April 13, 1993. *Academe The Week* listed on the Internet. First-week connections: 9,000.

October 1993. Fifth anniversary issue of *The Chronicle of Philanthropy*. Number of editorial staff: 15. Circulation: 30,066.

Fall 1993. Production of sales video. First all-glossy *Events in Academe*.

Appendix B

Interview Subjects

The Chronicle of Higher Education:

Primary contacts:

Corbin Gwaltney, Editor

Malcolm G. Scully, Managing Editor

Edward R. Weidlein, Associate Editor

Philip W. Semas, former Managing Editor of *The Chronicle of Higher Education* and currently Editor of *The Chronicle of Philanthrophy*

Secondary contacts:

Associate Publishers: William D. Criger, Joyce Hackley Giusto, Robinette D. Ross.

Associate Managing Editors: Cheryl M. Fields (*Point of View & Opinion*), Paul Desruisseaux (*International*), Scott Jaschik (*National*).

Senior Editors: Douglas Lederman (*Athletics* and Special Projects); Rose Engelland (Photography); Peter H. Stafford (Art Director); and Edith U. Taylor (*Gazette*).

Senior Writers: Lawrence Biemiller, Ellen K. Coughlin, Robert L. Jacobson.

Associate Senior Editor: Gail Lewin.

Comptroller: Thomas M. Beauchamp

Office Manager: Lisa Birchard.

Other contacts:

Robert Atwell, President, American Council on Education, Washington, D. C.

Terrel Bell, President of Terrel Bell & Associates, Salt Lake City, Utah. Former Secretary of Education. Author, *The Thirteenth Man*.

Ernest Boyer, President, Carnegie Foundation for the Advancement of Teaching, Princeton, New Jersey.

Howard Bray, Director, Knight Center for Specialized Journalism, College of Journalism, University of Maryland, College Park, Maryland.

Wendy Bresler, Editor, *Educational Record*, American Council on Education, Washington, D. C.

Shirley Chater, President, Texas Woman's University, Denton, Texas. (Subsequently became Commissioner of Society Security Administration.)

Reese Cleghorn, President, *American Journalism Review*, and Dean, College of Journalism, University of Maryland, College Park, Maryland.

John Crowl, retired partner/publisher, *The Chronicle of Higher Education*, South Woodstock, Vermont.

Russell Edgerton, President, American Association for Higher Education, and Chairman of the Editorial Group, Washington, D. C.

William C. Friday, President Emeritus, University of North Carolina, Chapel Hill, N.C. Co-chairman, Knight Commission on Intercollegiate Athletics.

Fred Hechinger, Senior Adviser, Carnegie Corporation of New York, former higher education reporter, the *New York Times*

Clark Kerr, President Emeritus, University of California, Berkeley, California.

Theodore J. Marchese, Executive Editor, *Change* Magazine, and Vice President, American Association for Higher Education, Washington, D. C.

Allan Ostar, former president, American Association of State Colleges and Universities, Washington, D. C.; currently higher education consultant and senior consultant for Academic Search Consultation Service, Washington, D,C,

Alan Pifer, former president, Carnegie Corporation of New York, Southport, Connecticut.

David Riesman, Harvard social scientist; former member, Carnegie Commission on Higher Education, Winchester, Massachusetts.

Lisa J. Walker, Executive director, Education Writers Association, Washington, D. C.

Ronald Wolk, Chairman, Editorial Projects in Education, Washington, D. C.

APPENDIX C

THE CHRONICLE OF HIGHER EDUCATION

EMPLOYEES, 1966-1991

Based on a poster prepared for the newspaper's 25th anniversary.

1966
Corbin Gwaltney*
Jack Crowl*
Bill Miller
Peggy W. Parker
Nancy Jarboe Ruel
Charmayne Proffitt
Paulette Duda
Ian McNett
Jim Brann
Barbara Field
Bob Jacobson
Anne Anderson

1967
Bob Ciapetta
Virginia Benson
Terry Easton

Linda Harman
Ann Graham
Pamela Brown
Malcolm Scully*

1968
Betty Funk
Joan Abell
Laura Donaldson
Susan Pralgaver
Claudia Groh
Diane Rosen
Susan McElhinney
Mary Plantinga

1969
Cliff Payne
Barbara Rohde

Monika Kranich
Claudia Keith
Phil Semas*
Catherine Mlinarchik
Merry Clark
Bonnie Camp
Gene Gall
Paula Gaines
Tony Jones
Ab Logan

1970

Cheryl Fields*
Anne Mommers
Jean Bolton
Muriel Walcutt
Dennis Cogswell
Louise Eberly
Dedie Uunila Taylor*
Brenda Alford
Margaret Tolson
Elisabeth Mason
Liz Prasad
Linda Smith
Bill Sievert
Susan Kaufmann
Marilyn Storch
Thelma Brown

1971

Andrea Schiff
Delores Shade
Nancy Alsfelder
Sally Donohue
Ted Weidlein*
Jacqueline Adams

Diana Dickey
Larry Van Dyne
Amanda Spake
Marc Goloven
Peter Janssen

1972

Jean C. Gwaltney
Tinney Humphreys
John Holland
Valerie French
Theresa Ebert
Alexdra Feeman Stevens
James Weidlein
Karen Winkler*
Sara Viviano Dodd
Meg Gwaltney
Margie Weeks

1973

Phil Boffey
Barbara Johnson
Susan Hadler
Cynthia Stanley
Janina Dawson Valaer
Janice Dunbar
Linda Johnson
Peggy J. Parker
Beverly Watkins*
Jack Magarrell
Natalie Davis Spingarn

1974

Michael Lane
Christopher Finan
Susan Morris

Rose Gaines
Faye Washington
Kevin King
Diana Quinn
Amy Malik
Susan Paul
Joan Maneri
Marcelle Sussman
Meryl Bland

1975
Catherine Bauman
Rachel Hughes
Anne McElaney
Karne Calbert
Terri Willis
Anita Tomikel
Jerry Lindgren*
Howard Means
Mickey Logue
Melanie Marsh
Ellen Coughlin*
Daniel Greenberg
Gael O'Brien
Elisabeth Rosenthal
Tina Wuelfing
Chiquitta Costner
Steve Smith*

1976
Charles Hollway
Marion O'Brien
Patricia Gibbs
John Burton
Susan Linowitz
Irene Wozny
Don Vannoy

Howard Wuelfing
Anne Roark
Pam Innburgia
Jane Kennedy
Karin Kiewra
Michael Staub
Betsy Reich

1977
Kirsti Uunila
Tracy O'Connor
Sue Brown
Ann Miller
Sarah Jacobs
Maureen Markey
Catherine Shea
Fran DeMouy
John Phillips
Adrienne Masters
Christopher Wienert
Victoria Mlynar
Amy Kirshbaum
Pamela Leary
Catherine Seigerman

1978
Robinette Davis Ross*
Karen Rogers
Zoe Ingalls
Celia Grail
Jane Lindquist
Jeffrey Cohen
Evangeline Horton
Lorenzo Middleton
Nancy Lay
Sarah Haft
John Borstel

Sandra Suominen
Herb Watzman
Prudence Fenton
Adrian Masters
Donna Shoemaker
Audrey Cowgill
Catherine O'Neill
Christine Higgs
Richard Muringer
Amy Longsworth
Barbara McKenna
Betsy Jacobs Hunt
Karen Heyl
Noreen McGrath
Mary Jo Otsea
Kathy Dominicis

1979
Margaret Paynter
Grace Paine
Gaal Shepherd
JoAnn Hutcheson
Sheppard Ranbom
Bill Brumby
Ericka Fredericks*
Linda Bullock
Stephen Davis
Sampath Ramaswami
Rebecca Birkel
Laura Snowden Harris*
Catherine Myers
Mark Jenkins
Lisa Birchard*
Pete Stafford*
Shelley Hoddinott
Laura Godfrey
Janet Hook

Frances Hull Oxholm*
Joyce Hackley Giusto*
Stacy Baenen

1980
Theresa Kilcarr
Kathleen Selvaggio
Kevin Whitcombe
Catherine Clements
Karen Heyl
Jeffrey Ranbom
Tyler Feather Whitmore*
Peter Bureau
Mary Jordan
Angela Petrillo*
Mary Ellen Biesiadecki
Angus Paul
Jeffery Patrick
Sally Sachar
Michelle McCarthy
Lawrence Biemiller*
Susan Robinson
Nina Martin
Greg Steinke
Sharon Varley
John Calcagno
Ann Jones
Marilil Kassab
Anne Milar Wiebe*

1981
Robert Banks
Laura Murphy
Lisa Holton
Laura Fortenbaugh
Julie Edgeworth
Nancy Gardner

Brenda Appleby
Joan Costa
John Garver
Susan Littlefield
Judith Nagy
Sharon Schindler
Amy Harbison
Pamela White
Jeffrey Ogden
Thomas Kunz
Donna Deaton*
Dinny Moses
Angela Carter
Laura Crosslin
Kim McDonald*
Jeanne Gorman
Donna Simmons
Vaughn Abbott
Grossie Smith
Bill Criger*

1982

Etta Solomon
Maria Rudensky
Beth Haiken
Nina Ayoub*
Paul Desruisseaux*
Elissa Shaw
Doris Flowers
Ronnie Jacobson
Patrick Crowl
Suzanne Perry
Scott Vance
Martha Dudrow
Ralph Chittams
Charles Farrell

Stacy Palmer*
Angela Dicianna

1983

Betsy Barefoot*
Anna Manville
Taryn Tora
Mary Davies
Peter Monaghan*
Kathlene Collins
Judith Axler Turner*
Karen Crowner
Sherrill Hudson
Tony Kaye
Greg Evans
Sue LaLumia*
Mary Scanlan Allison*
Catherine Spillman
Barbara Kraft
Jean Evangelauf*
Katharine Smeallie
Rose Engelland*
Angela Puryear*
Marianne Williams Jacobs*
Donna Engelgau
Susan Lothers*

1984

Scott Heller*
Margaret Petrie
Stephanie Cooper
Marie Engel Earnhart*
Cathy Hosley*
Patricia Newell
Liz Greene*
Meg Magill Connolly*

Claudia Saladin
Tom Meyer
Stephanie Croyder
Tracy Armstrong
Liz McMillen
Gaynelle Evans

1985

Jasmine Stewart*
Barton Hosley*
Ann Davant
Linda Silverstein
Carole Griffin
Karen Steinke
Ellen Treger Wilson*
Graciela Ferlito
Mario Ferlito*
Gwen Lappley*
Joan Amatniek
Gail Swanson
Susan Stewart
Carol Petrie
Anne Beck
Christian Crumlish
Robin Wilson*
Scott Jaschik*
Cindy Kennedy*
Anne Washington
Elizabeth Blair
Debbie Bossard
Lynn Peebles
Linda Barrabee
Patricia McNaughton
Meredith Zimmerman

1986

Caitlin Kenny
Sarah Patton
Catherine Gunn
Colleen Cordes
Kolli Cates
Jojo Gragasin*
Jennifer Galloway
Jennifer Koberstein
Elizabeth Magill
Anne Lowrey Bailey*
Carolyn Mooney*
Kristen Pedisich*
David Wheeler*
Esther Washington*
Elisabeth Trowbridge
Charlie Hartley
Carol King*
Doug Lederman*
Kristyn Turaj
Emilie Woodward
Michele Collison*
Michael Hirschorn
Holly Horner*

1987

Katie Mangan*
Lisa Morris
Carolyn Robinson
Karen Piggott
Courtney Leatherman*
Brad White
Verria Neal*
Catherine Caton
Reggie Finnie
Michelle Mantz

Audrey Thomas
Jeanette Zuijdijk Puranen*
Jeanine Natriello
John Davis
Tom DeLoughry*
Diana Fishlock
Barbara Papendorp*
Cheryl Maupin
Brian Manning*
Gail Lewin*
Ted Benson*
Johanna Cross*
Anastasia Orfanoudis
Patricia Cateura
Mary Dempster
Susan Oberlander Dodge*
Stephen Richards

1988

Antonina Musgrove
Debra Blum*
Goldie Blumenstyk*
Sean Wood
Sabayna Ballard
Pegeen McGlathery*
David Schenk
Teri Allbright
Merin Wexler
Ellen Verdon*
Tom Morre
Merry Hayes
Garry Boulard
Lauren Coffman*
Ann Driscoll*
Gil Fuchsberg
Amanda Maguire
Lynn Mundell*

Joyce Phinisee*
Lora Thompson*
Kristin Goss*
Peter Fisher
Sharon Flinker
Johnny Moore
Eric Piccione
William Montague
Reed Cochran
Denise Magner*
Jane Welsh
Elise Banduccie
Stephen Green*
Elizabeth Klein
Wendy Melillo
Vince Stehle*
Ray Kiah
Susan McCray*
Julie Modes
Kelly O'Brien
LeRai Carter
Zoe Dictrow*
Jocelyn Hallazgo

1989

Mary Crystal Cage*
Holly Hall*
Chris Raymond*
Tim Steele*
Brenda Walter Hulme*
Chris Meyers
Genia Nethmann Hill*
Patricia Valdes*
Rosha Peavy*
Pam Poolson*
Carlos Solis
Debario Fleming

Opal Gazdik
Daniel Moran
Jennifer Hoffman Moore*
Daniel Turner
Lynn Galkoski*
Betsy Burkhardt
Edna Dumas
Annice Hirt
Peggy Kelly
Julie Nicklin*
Felicia Rice
Jean Wegimont
Karen Grassmuck*
Esperanza Paredes*
Thaddaeus Thomas
Bruce Millar*
Johanna Rodriguez*
Opal Rouse
Anne St. Vil*
Sherrie Good*
Richard Palmer
Sarah Huff Barton*
Darin Keesler

1990

Marty Michaels*
Charles Short*
Pamela Barton*
Day Wilkes*
Jonathan Gubits
Samuel Eziemefe*
Jean Rosenblatt*
Maureen Freimuth
Ellen Nash
Debbie Aurigemma*
Jennifer Wong
Tracey Dawkins

Colette Ah-Tye
Deanna Hornicek
Joe Pagels*
Ben Schonberger
Grant Williams*
Jill Braunstein
Anna Semas
Jennifer Leffler*
Ruby Miles
Bonnie Gaskins*
Bruce Wilson*

1991

David Miller*
Claudia Grinius
Donna Duggan
Beth McLaughlin
Robert Goldstone
David Wilson*
Esther Huff
Jaemin Kim
Erica Antonelli*
Renee Edwards
Jennifer Liston*
Sara Sklaroff
Martha Turner
Michael Brown*
Leisle Moody*
Gene Puryear*
Shazia Amin*
Kevin Hart*
Nichele McCoy*
Chris Ott*
Stacey Cramp*
Mia Michaux*
Stephen Burd*
Robert Schmidt, Jr.*

* still with newspaper at 25th anniversary

APPENDIX D

THE CHRONICLE OF HIGHER EDUCATION

International Correspondents, September 1993

Taken from the listing in the Sept. 22, 1993 issue of *The Chronicle.*

Argentina: Cristina Bonasegna

Australia: Geoffrey Maslen

Brazil: Daniela Hart

Britain: David Walker

Canada: Jennifer Lewington

Central America: Claudia Kolker

Chile: Tim Frasca

China: Nick Driver

Colombia: Leslie Gaye Wirpsa

Eastern Europe: Burton Bollag, Dusko Doder, Colin Woodard

France: Patricia Brett

Germany: Taryn Toro

Indonesia: Margot Cohen

Ireland: John Walshe

Israel: Herbert M. Watzman

Kenya: Robin Lubbock

Mexico: Rhona Statland de Lopez

Peru: Douglass Stinson

Russia: Gregory Gransden

South Africa: Linda Vergnani

Switzerland: Kirsten Gallagher

Spain: Justin Webster

REFERENCES

Ad age 300, The. (1993, June 14). *Advertising Age*, p. S-1-22.

Advertisement. (1993, January 8). *The Times Higher Education Supplement*, p. 38.

After the upheaval: How events in the Soviet Union are affecting Russia, the Baltics, exchange programs, and collaborative research. (1991, September 4). *The Chronicle of Higher Education*, pp. A54–57.

American U. of Beirut expects to open next month. (1992, September 1). *The Chronicle of Higher Education*, p. 29.

Answers to questions asked by Chinese students in U.S. (1989, June 21). *The Chronicle of Higher Education*, p. A31.

Anti-War anger flares anew. (1972, May 8). *The Chronicle of Higher Education*, p. 12.

Ask the professor. (1990, September 19). *The Chronicle of Higher Education*, p. B4.

Assembly on university goals and governance, The. (1975, Winter). *Daedalus*, pp. 322–347.

Atwell, R. (1993, January 15). President. American Council on Education. Interview by author. Washington, D.C.

Baldwin, P. (1992, July 11). Collegiate paper is font of information. *The Dallas Morning News*, pp. 1F–2F.

Beauchamp, T. M. (1993, September 23). Comptroller. *The Chronicle of Higher Education*. Interview by author. Washington, D.C.

Bedell, D. (1986, November 16). Pressure on the presidents: Sports scandals in college on chiefs' laps. *The Dallas Morning News*, pp. 1A, 20–21A.

Bell, T. H. (1988). *The Thirteenth Man*. New York: Free Press.

Bell, T. H. (1993, September 1). President. Terrel Bell & Associates. Salt Lake City, UT. Telephone interview by author.

Biemiller, L. (1985, December 4). The last weeks of an AIDS sufferer at Berkeley: a friend remembers. *The Chronicle of Higher Education*, pp. 1, 34.

Biemiller, L. (1993a, April 21). Helping divas from Modesto breathe new life into the musical theater. *The Chronicle of Higher Education*, p. A51.

Biemiller, L. (1993b, June 7). Senior writer. *The Chronicle of Higher Education*. Interview by author. Washington, D.C.

Birchard, L. (1993, January 14). Office manager. *The Chronicle of Higher Education*. Interview by author. Washington, D.C.

Black-college presidents plan a 'summit' amid displeasure with lobbying group. (1992, January 15). *The Chronicle of Higher Education*, p. A1, A29.

Bloom, A. (1987). *The Closing of the American Mind*. New York: Simon and Schuster.

Boffey, P. M. (1974, June 10). Revelation of falsified research results shakes Sloan-Kettering. *The Chronicle of Higher Education*, p. 7.

Bornmann, J. A. (1971, November 1). Year's surveillance of lecturers? [*Letter to the Editor*]. *The Chronicle of Higher Education*, p. 6.

Bowler, M. (1988, Spring). Why the media doesn't tell your story. *Educational Record*, pp. 9–13.

Boyer, E. L. (1987). *College: The Undergraduate Experience in America*. New York: Harper & Row.

Boyer, E. L. (1993, July 12). President. Carnegie Foundation for the Advancement of Teaching. Princeton, NJ. Telephone interview by author.

Brann, J. W. (1968, April 15). Colleges' Negro-aid activities spurred by Dr. King's death. *The Chronicle of Higher Education*, pp. 1, 5.

Branson, L. (1989, May 31). Tiananmen Square, the center of Chinese power, becomes the symbol of China's confusion. *The Chronicle of Higher Education*, pp. A27–29.

Bray, H. (1993, June 8). Director. Knight Center for Specialized Journalism. College of Journalism. University of Maryland. Interview by author. College Park, MD.

Bresler, W. (1993, June 10). Editor. *Educational Record.* American Council on Education. Interview by author. Washington, D.C.

Budd, J. M. (1990). Higher education literature: Characteristics of citation patterns. *Journal of Higher Education*, 61(1), 84–97.

Budd, J. M. (1992, November 11). Associate professor. Louisiana State University. Baton Rouge, LA. Telephone interview by author.

Chater, S. (1993, August 24). President. Texas Woman's University. Interview by author. Denton, TX.

Chinese intellectuals' May 16 statement in support of the student movement. (1989, June 21). *The Chronicle of Higher Education*, pp. A29–30.

Chronicle correspondent searched in Warsaw. (1985, March 6). *The Chronicle of Higher Education*, p. 35.

Classified advertising decreases at 19 trade periodicals in 1991. (1992, January). *Electronic Directory & Classified Report*, 6(1), 1–2.

Cleghorn, R. (1993, June 8). President. *American Journalism Review.* Dean. College of Journalism. University of Maryland. Interview by author. College Park, MD.

Cleveland, C. (1991, Spring-Summer). Grub Street in the groves of academe. *Gannett Center Journal*, 5(2–3), pp. 92–103.

Connell, C., and Yarrington, R. (1983, November/December). Everything you always wanted to know about *The Chronicle of Higher Education. Change*, pp. 11–27.

Coughlin, E. K. (1992, December 15). Senior writer. *The Chronicle of Higher Education.* Interview by author. Washington, D.C.

Criger, W. D. (1992, December 14). Associate publisher. *The Chronicle of Higher Education.* Interview by author. Washington, D.C.

Criger, W. D. (1993, September 23). Associate publisher. *The Chronicle of Higher Education*. Interview by author. Washington, D.C.

Crowl, J. A. (1969, September 29). 'Black studies' demands force debate over basic academic issues. *The Chronicle of Higher Education*, p 4.

Crowl, J. A. (1993, May 18). Retired publisher. *The Chronicle of Higher Education*. South Woodstock, VT. Telephone interview by author.

Currie, B. F. (1975, Summer). The emergence of a specialized newspaper: *The Chronicle of Higher Education* from 1966 to date. *Journalism Quarterly*, 52(2), 321–325.

DeLoughry, T. J. (1988, March 16). Students shut down university for the deaf, force newly named president to resign. *The Chronicle of Higher Education*, p. A1, A18.

Desruisseaux, P. (1983, September 14). Its sacked campus patrolled by guardsmen, Salvadoran University survives in 'exile.' *The Chronicle of Higher Education*, pp. 27–28.

Desruisseaux, P., Scully, M. G., and Zille, H. (1986, June 11). South Africa: The crisis, the campuses, and some messages from Africans. *The Chronicle of Higher Education*, pp. 1–20.

Desruisseaux, P. (1992, December 14). Associate managing editor (*International*). *The Chronicle of Higher Education*. Interview by author. Washington, D.C.

D'Souza, D. (1991). *Illiberal Education: The Politics of Race & Sex on Campus*. New York: Random House Inc.

Dugger, R. (1974, October 15). High noon in Texas. *The Chronicle of Higher Education*, p. 16.

Edgerton, R. (1993, January 15). President. American Association for Higher Education. Interview by author. Washington, D.C.

Education secretary calls for fundamental changes in colleges; ACE president hits 'guns over butter.' (1986, October 15.) *The Chronicle of Higher Education*, pp. 1, 26.

Ehrhart, W. (1971, November 29). But the pace comes. *The Chronicle of Higher Education*, p. 8.

End Paper. (1987a, November 4). To Derek Bok, after receiving an honorary doctorate at Harvard, 1973. *The Chronicle of Higher Education*, p. B60.

End Paper. (1987b, November 11). For the student strikers. *The Chronicle of Higher Education*, p. B60.

Engelland, R. (1993, January 14). Senior editor (Photography). *The Chronicle of Higher Education*. Interview by author. Washington, D.C.

Fields, C. M. (1971, March 22). Federal probes into sex discrimination provoke controversy on campus. *The Chronicle of Higher Education*, p. A1.

Fields, C. M., and Hook, J. (1981, January 26). Bell promises a 'dramatic change' in views on college desegregation. *The Chronicle of Higher Education*, p. 1, 12.

Fields, C. M. (1993, January 14). Associate managing editor. (*Point of View & Opinion*). *The Chronicle of Higher Education*. Interview by author. Washington, D.C.

For minority Americans abroad, challenges transcend the academic. (1992, November 25). *The Chronicle of Higher Education*, pp. A27, A30.

Friday, W. C. (1993, August 25). President emeritus. University of North Carolina. Chapel Hill, N.C. Telephone interview by author.

Giusto, J. H. (1993, September 23). Associate publisher. *The Chronicle of Higher Education*. Interview by author. Washington, D.C.

Grassmuck, K. (1991, August 7). Stanford's Kennedy to step down in effort to end the controversy on overhead costs. *The Chronicle of Higher Education*, pp. A1, A10.

Graubard, S. R. (1970, Summer). Preface to the issue "Rights and responsibilities: The university's dilemma." *Daedalus*, 99(3), v–xiv.

Gwaltney, C. (1966, July 3). Big issues in higher education. Paper presented at the national conference of the American Alumni Council, San Francisco, CA.

Gwaltney, C. (1967, January 27). The dismissal of Clark Kerr—And his new assignment. *The Chronicle of Higher Education*, pp. 1, 6.

Gwaltney, C. (1969, August). *The Chronicle of Higher Education*: An analysis. Unpublished study.

Gwaltney, C. (1992a, September 11). Editor. *The Chronicle of Higher Education*. Washington, D.C. Telephone interview by author.

Gwaltney, C. (1992b, September 18). Editor. *The Chronicle of Higher Education*. Washington, D.C. Telephone interview by author.

Gwaltney, C. (1992c, October 2). Editor. *The Chronicle of Higher Education*. Washington, D.C. Telephone interview by author.

Gwaltney, C. (1992d, October 9). Editor. *The Chronicle of Higher Education*. Washington, D.C. Telephone interview by author.

Gwaltney, C. (1992e, October 23). Editor. *The Chronicle of Higher Education*. Washington, D.C. Telephone interview by author.

Gwaltney, C. (1992f, October 30). Editor. *The Chronicle of Higher Education*. Washington, D.C. Telephone interview by author.

Gwaltney, C. (1992g, November 6). Editor. *The Chronicle of Higher Education*. Washington, D.C. Telephone interview by author.

Gwaltney, C. (1992h, November 13). Editor. *The Chronicle of Higher Education*. Washington, D.C. Telephone interview by author.

Gwaltney, C. (1992i, December 4). Editor. *The Chronicle of Higher Education*. Washington, D.C. Telephone interview by author.

Gwaltney, C. (1992j, December 11). Editor. *The Chronicle of Higher Education*. Washington, D.C. Telephone interview by author.

Gwaltney, C. (1992k, December 14). Editor. *The Chronicle of Higher Education*. Interview by author. Washington, D.C.

Gwaltney, C. (1992l, December 15). Editor. *The Chronicle of Higher Education*. Interview by author. Washington, D.C.

Gwaltney, C. (1993a, January 8). Editor. *The Chronicle of Higher Education*. Washington, D.C. Telephone interview by author.

Gwaltney, C. (1993b, January 22). Editor. *The Chronicle of Higher Education*. Washington, D.C. Telephone interview by author.

Gwaltney, C. (1993c, February 12). Editor. *The Chronicle of Higher Education*. Washington, D.C. Telephone interview by author.

Gwaltney, C. (1993d, February 26). Editor. *The Chronicle of Higher Education*. Washington, D.C. Telephone interview by author.

Gwaltney, C. (1993e, March 12). Editor. *The Chronicle of Higher Education*. Washington, D.C. Telephone interview by author.

Gwaltney, C. (1993f, March 26). Editor. *The Chronicle of Higher Education*. Washington, D.C. Telephone interview by author.

Gwaltney, C. (1993g, April 23). Editor. *The Chronicle of Higher Education*. Washington, D.C. Telephone interview by author.

Gwaltney, C. (1993h, May 7). Editor. *The Chronicle of Higher Education*. Washington, D.C. Telephone interview by author.

Gwaltney, C. (1993i, May 21). Editor. *The Chronicle of Higher Education*. Washington, D.C. Telephone interview by author.

Gwaltney, C. (1993j, June 7). Editor. *The Chronicle of Higher Education*. Interview by author. Washington, D.C.

Gwaltney, C. (1993k, June 8). Editor. *The Chronicle of Higher Education*. Interview by author. Washington, D.C.

Gwaltney, C. (1993l, June 9). Editor. *The Chronicle of Higher Education*. Interview by author. Washington, D.C.

Gwaltney, C. (1993m, June 10). Editor. *The Chronicle of Higher Education*. Interview by author. Washington, D.C.

Gwaltney, C. (1993n, September 23). Editor. *The Chronicle of Higher Education*. Interview by author. Washington, D.C.

Gwaltney, C. (1993o, September 24). Editor. *The Chronicle of Higher Education*. Interview by author. Washington, D.C.

Gwaltney, C. (1993p, September 15). *Marginalia. The Chronicle of Higher Education*, p. A6.

Hechinger, F. (1993, August 19). Senior adviser. Carnegie Corporation of New York. New York, NY. Telephone interview by author.

Hefferlin, J. B., and Phillips, E. L., Jr. (1971). *Information Services for Academic Administration*. San Francisco: Jossey-Bass Inc.

Heller, Scott. (1984, November 14). Social pressures and new local laws forcing colleges to limit smoking. *The Chronicle of Higher Education*, p. 23.

Herbst, R. (1993, May 27). 'Instant' gardens with a wild look. *The New York Times*, pp. C1, C10.

Hook, Janet. (1980, September 29). Renovations for handicapped students cost less than expected, colleges find. *The Chronicle of Higher Education*, p. 15.

Howard, B. (1989, May 10). In "Epitaphs for the Living,' a photographer links words and images in a time of AIDS. *The Chronicle of Higher Education*, p. B1.

Ingalls, Z. (1986, September 3). As Harvard marks its birthday this week, U.S. higher education enters its 351st year. *The Chronicle of Higher Education*, pp. 1, 65.

Jacobson, R. L. (1989, June 14). Beijing University, before and after. *The Chronicle of Higher Education*, pp. A34–35.

Jacobson, R. L. (1993, June 9). Senior writer. *The Chronicle of Higher Education*. Interview by author. Washington, D.C.

Jaschik, S. (1986, September 3). A governor pours millions more into education. *The Chronicle of Higher Education*, p. 25.

Jaschik, S. (1992, January 8). President of black-college lobbying group stirs furor with claim ACE is racist. *The Chronicle of Higher Education*, pp. 1A, 37A.

Jaschik, S. (1993, February 26). Associate managing editor (National). *The Chronicle of Higher Education*. Washington, D.C. Telephone interview by author.

Jones, W. H. (1970a, March 16). U.S. lack of scholarly competence on Vietnam is called a scandal. *The Chronicle of Higher Education*, pp. 1, 4–5.

Jones, W. H. (1970b, May 11). Diary of a tense night at a Yale 'command post.' *The Chronicle of Higher Education*, pp. 1, 6.

Jordan, M. (1992, June 21). Profs and losses: Pressures are leading college heads to quit. *The Dallas Morning News*, pp. 1A, 20A.

Kerr, C. (1968). New challenges to the college and university. In K. Gordon (Ed.), *Agenda for the Nation* (pp. 237–276). Washington, D.C.: Brookings Institution.

Kerr, C. (1993, June 25). President emeritus. University of California. Interview by author. Berkeley, CA.

Lagemann, E. C. (1983). *Private Power for the Public Good: A History of the Carnegie Foundation for the Advancement of Teaching.* Middletown, Conn.: Wesleyan University Press.

Lane, C. M. (1985, September 11). Peru's universities starting to crack under pressures. *The Chronicle of Higher Education,* pp. 85–86.

Lecca, P. J. (1992, January 22). Charges of racism against the ACE's president. [*Letter to the Editor*]. *The Chronicle of Higher Education,* p. B4.

Lederman, D. (1992a, July 22). Survey suggests many Division I colleges fail to graduate their black athletes. *The Chronicle of Higher Education,* pp. A31–38.

Lederman, D. (1992b, December 15). Senior editor (*Athletics* and Special Projects). *The Chronicle of Higher Education.* Interview by author. Washington, D.C.

Lederman, D. (1993b, May 5). Colleges comply, but not happily, with 1987 law. *The Chronicle of Higher Education,* p. A14.

Lewin, G. (1993, January 14). Associate senior editor. *The Chronicle of Higher Education.* Interview by author. Washington, D.C.

Magazine called *Change* set to begin in January. (1968, September 23). *The Chronicle of Higher Education,* p. 6.

Maisel, I. (1991, March 20). Colleges need control, report says. *The Dallas Morning News,* pp. 1B, 9B.

Mangan, K. S. (1990, April 18). Pursuing a mission to support Hispanics before, during, and after the college years. *The Chronicle of Higher Education,* p. A3.

Mangan, K. S. (1991, October 23). Texas professor loses honors-program post. *The Chronicle of Higher Education,* p. A15.

Marchese, T. J. (1993, June 7). Executive editor. *Change.* Vice president. American Association for Higher Education. Interview by author. Washington, D.C.

Marginalia. (1978, October 2). *The Chronicle of Higher Education,* p. 2.

Marginalia. (1986, December 17). *The Chronicle of Higher Education,* p. 2.

McBee, S. (1979, February 20). Reporter is cited for GSA articles. *The Washington Post*, p. A20.

McDonald, K. (1982, July 14). State nursing school may not bar men, Supreme Court rules in 5-to-4 vote. *The Chronicle of Higher Education*, pp. 1, 12.

McDonald, K., and Vance, N. S. (1982, September 1). Colleges urged to teach athletes, coaches the dangers of drug abuse and 'doping.' *The Chronicle of Higher Education*, pp. 25–26, 28.

McDougall, P. (1993, September 15). *Folio* 500: The best and the biggest. *Folio*, pp. 53–69.

McMillen, L. (1992, December 16). How a journey of expediency became the stuff of legend: An anthropologist's ground-breaking 'accident.' *The Chronicle of Higher Education*, pp. A6–7.

McNett, Ian F. (1966, November 23). Politics and higher education: The picture changes for '67/Congress. *The Chronicle of Higher Education*, pp. 1, 5.

Merkowitz, David. (1993, June 2). Pay and benefits for the executives of academe. *The Chronicle of Higher Education*, p. B4.

Middleton, L. (1978, July 24). Welcome cools for Iranians on many campuses. *The Chronicle of Higher Education*, pp. 9–10.

Middleton, L. (1978, October 2). Black professors on white campuses: Despite progress, many still feel isolated and uncertain of the future in academe. *The Chronicle of Higher Education*, pp. 1, 8–12.

Molins, K. E., and Martin, T. D. (1987). Hiring practices in higher education. Survey report, Oxford College of Emory University, Oxford, GA.

North Carolina's college deal. (1981, July 2). *The New York Times*, p. 22.

North Carolina president has his say on CBS. (1981, October 7). *The Chronicle of Higher Education*, p. 2.

Ostar, A. (1993, June 7). Senior consultant. Academic Search Consultation Service. Interview by author. Washington, D.C.

Palmer, S. E. (1986, October 22). Campus officials assail Bennett's attack on colleges; Harvard's Bok calls secretary's analysis 'superficial.' *The Chronicle of Higher Education*, pp. 1, 17.

Phillips, J. C. (1978, January 16). A college of, by, and for Navajo Indians. *The Chronicle of Higher Education*, p. 10–12.

Pifer, A. (1993, June 16). Former president, Carnegie Corporation of New York. Southport, CT. Telephone interview by author.

Reese, W. (1966, November 23). Politics and higher education: The picture changes for '67/California. *The Chronicle of Higher Education*, pp. 1, 5.

Rein, R. K. (1973, April 30). Stock scandal said to involve 14 college funds. *The Chronicle of Higher Education*, p. 1, 8.

Rice, P. O., and Paster, A. L. (1990). Chronicling the academic library: Library news coverage by the *Chronicle of Higher Education*. *The Journal of Academic Librarianship*, 16(5), 285–290.

Riesman, D. (1950) *The Lonely Crowd: A Study of the Changing American Character*. New Haven: Yale University Press.

Riesman, D. (1993, August 24). Harvard University social scientist. Former member. Carnegie Commission on Higher Education. Winchester, MA. Telephone interview by author.

Ross, R. D. (1992, December 14). Associate publisher. *The Chronicle of Higher Education*. Interview by author. Washington, D.C.

Ross, R. D. (1993, February 12). Associate publisher. *The Chronicle of Higher Education*. Washington, D.C. Telephone interview by author.

Scully, M. G. (1970, February 9). Women in higher education: Challenging the status quo. *The Chronicle of Higher Education*, p. 2–5.

Scully, M. G. (1980, January 28). Carnegie panel says enrollment declines will create a 'new academic revolution.' *The Chronicle of Higher Education*, p. 1, 11.

Scully, M. G. (1992a, September 11). Managing editor. *The Chronicle of Higher Education*. Washington, D.C. Telephone interview by author.

Scully, M. G. (1992b, September 18). Managing editor. *The Chronicle of Higher Education*. Washington, D.C. Telephone interview by author.

Scully, M. G. (1992c, October 2). Managing editor. *The Chronicle of Higher Education*. Washington, D.C. Telephone interview by author.

Scully, M. G. (1992d, October 9). Managing editor. *The Chronicle of Higher Education*. Washington, D.C. Telephone interview by author.

Scully, M. G. (1992e, October 23). Managing editor. *The Chronicle of Higher Education*. Washington, D.C. Telephone interview by author.

Scully M. G. (1992f, October 30). Managing editor. *The Chronicle of Higher Education*. Washington, D.C. Telephone interview by author.

Scully, M. G. (1992g, November 6). Managing editor. *The Chronicle of Higher Education*. Washington, D.C. Telephone interview by author.

Scully, M. G. (1992h, November 13). Managing editor. *The Chronicle of Higher Education*. Washington, D.C. Telephone interview by author.

Scully, M. G. (1992i, December 4). Managing editor. *The Chronicle of Higher Education*. Washington, D.C. Telephone interview by author.

Scully, M. G. (1992j, December 11). Managing editor. *The Chronicle of Higher Education*. Washington, D.C. Telephone interview by author.

Scully, M. G. (1992k, December 14). Managing editor. *The Chronicle of Higher Education*. Interview by author. Washington, D.C.

Scully, M. G. (1992l, December 15). Managing editor. *The Chronicle of Higher Education*. Interview by author. Washington, D.C.

Scully, M. G. (1993a, January 8). Managing editor. *The Chronicle of Higher Education*. Washington, D.C. Telephone interview by author.

Scully, M. G. (1993b, January 14). Managing editor. *The Chronicle of Higher Education*. Interview by author. Washington, D.C.

Scully, M. G. (1993c, January 15). Managing editor. *The Chronicle of Higher Education*. Interview by author. Washington, D.C.

Scully, M. G. (1993d, January 22). Managing editor. *The Chronicle of Higher Education*. Washington, D.C. Telephone interview by author.

Scully, M. G. (1993e, February 12). Managing editor. *The Chronicle of Higher Education*. Washington, D.C. Telephone interview by author.

Scully, M. G. (1993f, February 26). Managing editor. *The Chronicle of Higher Education*. Washington, D.C. Telephone interview by author.

Scully, M. G. (1993g, March 12). Managing editor. *The Chronicle of Higher Education*. Washington, D.C. Telephone interview by author.

Scully, M. G. (1993h, March 26). Managing editor. *The Chronicle of Higher Education*. Washington, D.C. Telephone interview by author.

Scully, M. G. (1993i, April 23). Managing editor. *The Chronicle of Higher Education*. Washington, D.C. Telephone interview by author.

Scully, M. G. (1993j, May 7). Managing editor. *The Chronicle of Higher Education*. Washington, D.C. Telephone interview by author.

Scully, M. G. (1993k, May 21). Managing editor. *The Chronicle of Higher Education*. Washington, D.C. Telephone interview by author.

Scully, M. G. (1993l, June 7). Managing editor. *The Chronicle of Higher Education*. Interview by author. Washington, D.C.

Scully, M. G. (1993m, June 8). Managing editor. *The Chronicle of Higher Education*. Interview by author. Washington, D.C.

Scully, M. G. (1993n, June 9). Managing editor. *The Chronicle of Higher Education*. Interview by author. Washington, D.C.

Scully, M. G. (1993o, June 10). Managing editor. *The Chronicle of Higher Education*. Interview by author. Washington, D.C.

Semas, P. (1968, December 2). Violence plagues S. F. State; Race issues flare elsewhere. *The Chronicle of Higher Education*, pp. 1, 3.

Semas, P. (1975, March 24). Foreign students: More coming. *The Chronicle of Higher Education*, pp. 1, 8.

Semas, P. (1992a, October 9). Editor. *The Chronicle of Philanthropy*. Washington, D.C. Telephone interview by author.

Semas, P. (1992b, October 23). Editor. *The Chronicle of Philanthropy*. Washington, D.C. Telephone interview by author.

Semas, P. (1992c, December 14). Editor. *The Chronicle of Philanthropy*. Interview by author. Washington, D.C.

Semas, P. (1993a, February 12). Editor. *The Chronicle of Philanthropy*. Washington, D.C. Telephone interview by author.

Semas, P. (1993b, March 12). Editor. *The Chronicle of Philanthropy*. Washington, D.C. Telephone interview by author.

Sequence of events in tragedy at Kent State, with Scranton Panel's notes. (1970, November 9). *The Chronicle of Higher Education*, pp. 1, 4–5.

Seventeen leading trade periodicals are flat in 1990 classified advertising volume. (1991, January). *Classified Advertising Report*, 5(1), 1–2.

Stafford, P. H. (1993, June 9). Senior editor (Art Director). *The Chronicle of Higher Education*. Interview by author. Washington, D.C.

Stipp, D. (1992, September 11). The gender gap: Our schools make it hard for girls to pursue math and science. *The Wall Street Journal*, p. B8.

Taylor, E. U. (1992, December 14). Senior editor (*Gazette*). *The Chronicle of Higher Education*. Interview by author. Washington, D.C.

Thomas, A. E. (1992, January 22). Charges of racism against the ACE's president. [*Letter to the Editor*]. *The Chronicle of Higher Education*, p. B4.

Thornborough, T. (1990, August 15). Kuwait higher education troubled even before Iraq's invasion. *The Chronicle of Higher Education*, p. A27, 29.

Thorpe, J. (1972, February 22). Intercollegiate sports and women [*Letter to the Editor*]. *The Chronicle of Higher Education*, p. 8.

Thrower, R. (1970, March 30). Pressures, not revolt, said to have ousted Trenton State head [*Letter to the Editor*]. *The Chronicle of Higher Education*, p. 4.

Walker, L. J. (1993, August 31). Executive director. Education Writers Association, Washington, D.C. Telephone interview by author.

Watkins, Beverly T. (1980, June 9). 'Fallout' from the Yeshiva ruling. *The Chronicle of Higher Education*, p. 3.

Watzman, H. M. (1978, December 4). Stakes are high, political activity is low on Israel's campuses. *The Chronicle of Higher Education*, pp. 3–4.

Weidlein, E. R. (1992a, September 11). Associate editor. *The Chronicle of Higher Education*. Washington, D.C. Telephone interview by author.

Weidlein, E. R. (1992b, September 18). Associate editor. *The Chronicle of Higher Education*. Washington, D.C. Telephone interview by author.

Weidlein, E. R. (1992c, October 2). Associate editor. *The Chronicle of Higher Education*. Washington, D.C. Telephone interview by author.

Weidlein, E. R. (1992d, October 9). Associate editor. *The Chronicle of Higher Education*. Washington, D.C. Telephone interview by author.

Weidlein E. R. (1992e, October 23). Associate editor. *The Chronicle of Higher Education*. Washington, D.C. Telephone interview by author.

Weidlein, E. R. (1992f, October 30). Associate editor. *The Chronicle of Higher Education*. Washington, D.C. Telephone interview by author.

Weidlein, E. R. (1992g, November 6). Associate editor. *The Chronicle of Higher Education*. Washington, D.C. Telephone interview by author.

Weidlein, E. R. (1992h, November 13). Associate editor. *The Chronicle of Higher Education*. Washington, D.C. Telephone interview by author.

Weidlein, E. R. (1992i, December 4). Associate editor. *The Chronicle of Higher Education* Washington, D.C. Telephone interview by author.

Weidlein, E. R. (1992j, December 11). Associate editor. *The Chronicle of Higher Education*. Washington, D.C. Telephone interview by author.

Weidlein, E. R. (1992k, December 14). Associate editor. *The Chronicle of Higher Education*. Interview by author. Washington, D.C.

Weidlein, E. R. (1992l, December 15). Associate editor. *The Chronicle of Higher Education*. Interview by author. Washington, D.C.

Weidlein, E. R. (1993a, January 8). Associate editor. *The Chronicle of Higher Education*. Washington, D.C. Telephone interview by author.

Weidlein, E. R. (1993b, January 14). Associate editor. *The Chronicle of Higher Education*. Interview by author. Washington, D.C.

Weidlein, E. R. (1993c, January 15). Associate editor. *The Chronicle of Higher Education*. Interview by author. Washington, D.C.

Weidlein, E. R. (1993d, January 22). Associate editor. *The Chronicle of Higher Education*. Washington, D.C. Telephone interview by author.

Weidlein, E. R. (1993e, February 12). Associate editor. *The Chronicle of Higher Education*. Washington, D.C. Telephone interview by author.

Weidlein, E. R. (1993f, February 26). Associate editor. *The Chronicle of Higher Education*. Washington, D.C. Telephone interview by author.

Weidlein, E. R. (1993g, March 12). Associate editor. *The Chronicle of Higher Education*. Washington, D.C. Telephone interview by author.

Weidlein, E. R. (1993h, March 26). Associate editor. *The Chronicle of Higher Education*. Washington, D.C. Telephone interview by author.

Weidlein, E. R. (1993i, April 23). Associate editor. *The Chronicle of Higher Education.* Washington, D.C. Telephone interview by author.

Weidlein, E. R. (1993j, May 7). Associate editor. *The Chronicle of Higher Education.* Washington, D.C. Telephone interview by author.

Weidlein, E. R. (1993k, May 21). Associate editor. *The Chronicle of Higher Education.* Washington, D.C. Telephone interview by author.

Weidlein, E. R. (1993l, June 7). Associate editor. *The Chronicle of Higher Education.* Interview by author. Washington, D.C.

Weidlein, E. R. (1993m, June 8). Associate editor. *The Chronicle of Higher Education.* Interview by author. Washington, D.C.

Weidlein, E. R. (1993n, June 9). Associate editor. *The Chronicle of Higher Education.* Interview by author. Washington, D.C.

Weidlein, E. R. (1993o, June 10). Associate editor. *The Chronicle of Higher Education.* Interview by author. Washington, D.C.

Williams, J. H. (1973, February 12). Re: The second sex. *The Chronicle of Higher Education,* p. 16.

Winkler, K. J. (1975, December 8). The state of black studies: Reports of their demise are proving to be exaggerated. *The Chronicle of Higher Education,* p. 5.

Wolk, R. A. (1963). *Disseminating Information about Higher Education.* Baltimore: Editorial Projects for Education.

Wolk, R. A. (1992, September). *A Short History of Editorial Projects in Education.* (Available from Editorial Projects in Education, 4301 Connecticut Avenue, N.W., Suite 250, Washington, D.C. 20008.)

Wolk, R. A. (1993, January 15). Chairman. Editorial Projects in Education. Interview by author. Washington, D.C.

Yarrington, R. (1985, Winter). J-schools should encourage higher education writers. *Journalism Educator,* pp. 11–12.

INDEX